ESSENTIAL MESSAGES FROM GOD'S SERVANTS

masterWork®

Lessons from

LIVING THE EXTRAORDINARY LIFE

by Charles Stanley

THE FIVE LANGUAGES OF APOLOGY

by Gary Chapman & Jennifer Thomas

FALL 2008

LifeWay®
Biblical Solutions for Life

Ross H. McLaren

Editor in Chief

Wanda King

Interim Editor

Carolyn B. Gregory

Copy Editor

David Wilson

Graphic Designer

Melissa Finn

Lead Technical Specialist

Alan Raughton

Lead Adult Ministry Specialist

David Apple

Adult Ministry Specialist

Send questions/comments to

Editor, *MasterWork*

One LifeWay Plaza

Nashville, TN 37234-0175

Or make comments on the Web at

www.lifeway.com

Management Personnel

Bret Robbe, *Director*

Leadership and Adult Publishing

Ron Brown, Larry Dry, Ron Keck

Managing Directors

Leadership and Adult Publishing

David Francis, *Director*

Sunday School

Bill Craig, *Director*

Leadership and Adult Ministry

Gary Hauk, *Director Publishing*

LifeWay Church Resources

Lessons by Charles Stanley are condensed from *Living the Extraordinary Life: Nine Principles to Discover It* (Nashville: Thomas Nelson, Inc., 2005). Used by permission of Thomas Nelson, In All rights reserved.

Lessons by Gary Chapman and Jennifer Thomas are condensed from *The Five Languages of Apology* (Chicago: Northfie Publishing, 2006).© Gary Chapman and Jennifer Thomas. Used by permission. All rights reserved.

Unless otherwise noted, all Scripture quotations in the lessons from *Living the Extraordinary Life: Nine Principles to Discover It* are from the New American Standard Bible. Copyright © 1960, 1962, 1963, 1968, 1971, 1972, 1973, 1975, 1977, 1995 by The Lockman Foundation. Used by permission.

Unless otherwise indicated, all Scripture quotations in the lessons from *The Five Languages of Apology* and those marked NIV are from the *Holy Bible: New International Version.* Copyright © 1973, 1978, 1984 by International Bible Society. Used by permission of Zondervan Publishing House. All rights reserved.

Quotations in the "How to Become a Christian" article or those marked HCSB are taken from the *Holman Christian Standard Bible®,* copyright © 1999, 2000, 2001, 2002 by Holman Bible Publishers. Used by permission. Scripture quotations noted KJV are from the *King James Version.* Scripture quotations noted NKJV are from *The New King James Version.* Copyright © 1979, 1980, 1982 Thomas Nelson, Inc., Publishers. Scripture quotations noted NLV are from the *New Life Version.* Scripture quotations noted NLT are from the *New Living Translation,* copyright © 1971. Used by permission of Tyndale House Publishers, Inc., Wheaton, Illinois 60189. All rights reserved.

MasterWork: Essential Messages from God's Servants (ISSN 1542-703X, Item 005075042) is published quarterly by LifeWay Christian Resources of the Southern Baptist Convention, One LifeWay Plaza, Nashville, Tennessee 37234; Thom S. Rainer, President. © Copyright 2008 LifeWay Christian Resources of the Southern Baptist Convention.

For ordering or inquiries, visit *www.lifeway.com,* or write LifeWay Church Resources Customer Service, One LifeWay Plaza, Nashville, TN 37234-0113. For subscriptions or subscription address changes, e-mail *subscribe@lifeway.com,* fax (615) 251-5818, or write to the above address. For bulk shipments mailed quarterly to one address, e-mail *orderentry@lifeway.com,* fax (615) 251-5933, or write to the above address.

Printed in the United States of America.

Cover photo credit:
© Comstock Images/Jupiterimages Unlimited

table of Contents

Living the Extraordinary Life

Life in the twenty-first century is tough. The world is becoming increasingly volatile. Despite unprecedented technological, scientific, and educational advances, our society grows more fragile with each passing year. Institutional, cultural, and moral foundations upon which we have come to depend are rapidly decaying, and pressures inside and outside the home sometimes overwhelm us.

Are you wrestling against forces that seem out of your control? Is life's treadmill going faster than you are? If you answer yes, like most people today, you are running your own life, moving from crisis to crisis without slowing down. Does your life seem less than productive?

The Bible offers us numerous principles for living an extraordinary life. In these lessons I will address nine time-tested truths God reveals to us through Scripture and discuss how we as believers can live extraordinary lives. What is this extraordinary life? It is the life sustained by an inner peace and joy in the good times as well as the bad.

Charles Stanley

Charles Stanley

is pastor of the 16,000-member First Baptist Church in Atlanta, Georgia, and is head of the international In Touch® Ministries. He has twice been elected president of the Southern Baptist Convention and is known internationally from his radio and television program *In Touch*. His many best-selling books include *When the Enemy Strikes, Finding Peace, Seeking His Face, Success God's Way, Enter His Gates, The Source of My Strength, How to Listen to God,* and *Landmines in the Path of the Believer*.

Dr. Stanley received his bachelor of arts degree from the University of Richmond, his bachelor of divinity degree from Southwestern Baptist Theological Seminary, and his master's and doctor's degrees from Luther Rice Seminary.

AMY SUMMERS wrote the personal learning activities and teaching plans this study. Amy is an experienced writer for LifeWay Bible study curriculum. She and her family live in Arden, North Carolina.

ABOUT THIS STUDY

A principle is: (1) a basic truth or law; (2) a basic essential quality that determines behavior; (3) a rule or law concerning the functioning of natural phenomena (American Heritage Dictionary; www.bartleby.com).

How could any of those definitions apply to biblical principles? _____

Read Psalm 119:93. What did the psalmist say about the principles or precepts from God's Word? _____

_____

Prayer:
Dear Father, help me learn and live the nine principles from Your Word in these lessons so I can live the extraordinary life You intend for me. Amen.

master*Work:*
Essential Messages from God's Servants

• Designed for developing and maturing believers who desire to go deeper into the spiritual truths of God's Word.

• Ideal for many types of Bible study groups.

• A continuing series from leading Christian authors and their key messages.

• Based on LifeWay's well-known, interactive model for daily Bible study.

• The interspersed interactive personal learning activities **in bold type** are written by the writer identified on the Study Theme unit page.

• Teaching plans follow each lesson to help facilitators guide learners through lessons.

• Published quarterly.

Complete Surrender to God Brings Complete Life

day One

Are You Running from God's Love?

I heard a story that makes a profound point about surrender. Some time ago a radio station reported news of a stolen VW Bug in California. The police staged an intense search for the vehicle and the man who stole it, even to the point of making announcements on local radio stations to contact him. On the front seat of the stolen car sat a box of crackers that, unbeknownst to the thief, was laced with poison. The car's owner had intended to use the crackers as rat bait. You see, the police and the owner of the car were more interested in apprehending the thief in order to save his life than to recover the vehicle. But the thief, not realizing their intentions, fled from the very people who sought to help him.

The story illustrates an important truth. So often we run from God in order to escape His punishment, but what we are actually doing is eluding His rescue.

God is omniscient. He knows all about us. He knows what we have done in the past and will do in the future. The wondrous thing about God's love is that it never stops. He loves us the same today as He did yesterday, and His love for us will not change tomorrow.

> "It is God's unconditional love that changes us and brings lasting fulfillment."
> —Charles Stanley

Read Romans 5:5 in your Bible. How is God's love measured out to you?
❏ **Rationed out in drops** ❏ **Poured out in buckets**

With this truth in mind, we must ask why so many people end up living less-than-productive lives. The answer lies in our ability to accept and apply a crucial truth to our hearts—it is God's unconditional love that changes us and brings lasting fulfillment. Once we understand and accept that there is no greater love than the love of God, we will be ready to take the first step toward living the extraordinary life.

If you have never received Christ as your Savior, you can exchange your old way of living for a new, extraordinary life. Tell Him that you want His life to be yours, and accept His death on the cross as sufficient payment for your sins. In so doing, you agree with Him that there is nothing you can do in your own strength to save yourself. It is through faith in God's Son that you are saved.

Once you have done this, you are ready to begin with the basics of the Christian faith—becoming a wise steward of your time, thoughts, talents, and treasures. Commit your desires, hopes, and dreams to God, and you will be amazed at the way He works everything together for your good and His glory.

> "More than that, I count all things to be loss in view of the surpassing value of knowing Christ Jesus my Lord, for whom I have suffered the loss of all things, and count them but rubbish so that I may gain Christ" (Phil. 3:8, NASB).

Read Philippians 3:8 in the margin. Circle below what was of greatest value to Paul. Underline what is of greatest value to you.

Possessions   **Family**   **Knowing Christ**
            Job   **Security**

Why do so many people fail to know their Creator? To begin with, many individuals live in darkness, unaware that there is one true God whom Jesus Christ came to reveal. For some reason, they were never exposed to the preaching of the gospel—a problem more prevalent perhaps in non-Christian societies but in no way limited to them; it is even common inside the walls of many churches.

Another reason is lack of interest in God. With cell phones, televisions, radios, and computers, we are overwhelmed with information, but no wiser than we were without them. Convinced that access to information equals knowledge, we often replace true wisdom with trivia.

Further, knowing God involves a cost, and some people are simply unwilling to pay the price.

Do you really want to know God? The way to do that is by knowing Christ. Receive Him as your Savior, who paid your sin-debt in full. Then accept His invitation to spend time in private conversation—He wants your undivided attention for a little while.

day Two

Have You Drifted from God's Love?

It's possible that you have been a Christian for years, but for some reason you are experiencing unreality with God. Ask the Lord to surface anything in your life that you need to surrender to Him. Your devotion and trust may have drifted. If that is the case, you need to address this first. Pray for God to renew your heart and refresh your spirit as you seek His counsel for your life.

Read Psalm 51:10-12 in your Bible. In the margin write David's prayer in your own words to reflect the desire of your heart.

Never feel guilty for returning to the basics of your faith. Christian leaders have told me that when they find themselves at a point of dryness, they return to the basics of their faith in God. They take extra time to be alone with the Lord and listen for His encouragement. They practice being in His presence.

Read the following verses and state some of the basic fundamentals of your faith.
Proverbs 3:5-6 _____

Galatians 2:19-20 _____

John 15:4-5 _____

A peace and a rest abide deep within the lives of those who let go of selfish desires long enough to experience the reality of God's goodness. Learning to abide instead of striving teaches you to place your trust in someone who knows much more than you do about life and what is to come. Once you have experienced the goodness of God's love, you will never want to return to a life of striving and self-effort. You will want to know more about your Savior and how your life can more effectively reflect His love and grace to others.

> "Once you have experienced the goodness of God's love, you will never want to return to a life of striving and self-effort."
> —Charles Stanley

day Three

Fulfillment In Life

Fulfillment is the result of God's presence living within you through His indwelling Holy Spirit. All that you do in life should reflect His goodness and mercy. But how do you reach a point of true fulfillment?

First, you must realize that fulfillment is not a matter of position or power. It is a matter of loving God and allowing Him to love you. All you need in order to be fulfilled is Jesus Christ living within you. As a believer, you are God's beloved child—an heir to His throne. There is no higher calling than this, and there is no greater position than the place you hold in His family. Truthfully, as a Christian, you have both authority and power. Although at times life may seem to have lost its sense of excitement and you may no longer hopefully anticipate the future, you should not settle for less. You can be fulfilled right now.

> "Fulfillment is not a matter of position or power. It is a matter of loving God and allowing Him to love you."
> —Charles Stanley

God designed your life for His glory. Even before you knew Him personally, He knew you intimately: " 'For I know the plans that I have for you,' declares the LORD, 'plans for welfare and not for calamity to give you a future and a hope' " (Jer. 29:11). When we surrender ourselves to God, we exchange our thoughts, feelings, and desires for new ones.

Submit yourself to God. Fulfillment comes only when you decide to love God and give Him all of yourself. This does not mean that you settle for second best or stop doing what you have been trained to do. Instead, you come to a point where you ask God to use you to the fullest so others will come to know Him and experience His forgiveness and unconditional love. Those who have never discovered the wondrous joy that comes from loving and serving God have yet to experience His eternal fulfillment.

God has a great plan for your life—a life that is exceptional. When you trust and seek only Him, He will teach you how to live above your circumstances.

Your understanding of *who* you are is the rudder that directs nearly everything you do. Knowing who you are and who you were created to be will transform performance-based notions of self-worth into a certainty upheld by God's infinite love.

Who Am I?

John 1:12

John 15:15

Romans 8:1-2

1 Corinthians 3:16

2 Corinthians 1:21-22

Philippians 3:20

Colossians 1:13-14

Colossians 2:10

Read three of the Scriptures referenced in the margin under *Who Am I?* and fill in the blanks, declaring true statements about yourself if you are a Christian.

I am _____

I am _____

I am _____

Scripture tells us that if anyone is in Christ, he is a new creation; the old has gone, and the new has come (2 Cor. 5:17).

You are the creation of God's hands—His imprint is upon you, and He wants you to be a reflection of His glory and character: "We all, with unveiled face, beholding as in a mirror the glory of the Lord, are being transformed into the same image from glory to glory, just as from the Lord, the Spirit" (2 Cor. 3:18).

He wants you to understand why you were created (and then recreated through Christ) as well as your purpose in this life.

Why Am I Here?

Matthew 5:13-14

John 15:16

1 Corinthians 3:9

2 Corinthians 5:20

Ephesians 2:10

Philippians 1:5

Read two of the references listed in the margin under *Why Am I Here?* and fill in the blanks, declaring true statements about your purpose.

I am _____

I am _____

When you understand how beloved you are and the greatness of your purpose, you will be energized to live for God through His power.

Your identity is secure because of who lives inside you, not because of what you do. Few of us, if any, seek a mundane existence. Instead, we long to experience life in a grand way. The glut of reality TV shows is genuine evidence of people craving something bigger than the ordinary lives they lead. Because we want to grow emotionally and intellectually, we constantly seek new ways to expand our vision and enjoy life more. However, extreme sports challenges, exotic vacations, and hedonistic thrills promise more than they can deliver.

> "Your identity is secure because of who lives inside you, not because of what you do."— Charles Stanley

There is only one antidote for spiritual thirst. God also wants us to experience permanent fulfillment. He created us for excellence, and from His perspective, our lives represent infinite possibilities. No matter how many wrong turns we take, God knows how to redirect our lives and set us back on the right track. He is the One who extends opportunity after opportunity to us. In other words, He is the God of the second, third, fourth, and infinite chances.

day Four

How God Gets Our Attention, Part 1

Read Isaiah 30:21 in your Bible and record the promise God gave to His people.

_____

Because we are Christians, it is incumbent upon us to be savvy travelers, alert to our Master's voice as we journey through life. We must walk in the Spirit, which means being receptive and responsive to God's instruction, no matter how He chooses to speak. And we must know how to distinguish between His voice and the others that vie for our attention—the opinions of our peers, rebellious attitudes, or lust for the world.

All too often, the Lord's wisdom is muffled by the clamor of daily life. Sometimes we start out with God's agenda but get so far ahead of Him that we can no longer hear His voice. Preferring to do things our own way, we lose contact with our only true Guide.

God speaks to us primarily in four ways—through His Word, through His Holy Spirit, through another person, and through the circumstances in our lives.

Ideally we should be so attuned to His voice that we hear as soon as He speaks. Unfortunately we are not always spiritually "tuned in." For such situations, God has a number of ways to get our attention.

A RESTLESS SPIRIT

One of the simplest ways God gets our attention is by making us restless. When King Ahasuerus was unable to sleep, he ordered that the royal record books be read. As a result, he discovered his life had been saved by Esther's uncle. In wanting to honor Mordecai, the king unwittingly set in motion a chain of events that caused Haman's planned annihilation of the Jews to backfire (Esth. 6–7). The Jewish nation was spared because the king was alert when God gave him a restless spirit.

If you experience a restlessness deep within—something you sense but cannot quite identify—the wise thing to do is stop and pray, "Lord, are You trying to say something to me?" God does not work the same way in everyone's life, but I believe His primary method for getting my attention is by giving me a restlessness to show I need a change of direction. As I reread my old journal entries, a pattern emerges—every single time God was about to move me from one pastorate to another, I would become very restless for a few months. This is a very gentle method that God uses to correct our course.

A SPOKEN WORD

A second way that God gets our attention is by a word spoken through someone else. Wanting to give Eli the priest a message, the Lord woke young Samuel by calling his name (1 Sam. 3:4–8). At first, the boy did not realize it was the voice of his Lord. Eli had to instruct him to listen carefully because God had a special message for Samuel (v. 9). God used the priest to pass along a word of encouragement to the boy. In a similar way, God also had Eli's attention for the forthcoming message He would deliver through Samuel (vv. 11–18).

AN UNUSUAL BLESSING

A third way God speaks is the method most people prefer—by blessing us in an unusual way. The blessing might be related to spiritual growth, finances, home, work, or health. But God does not always choose this method. For those who turn away and refuse to depend on Him, a lavish blessing would likely result in greater independence and self-centeredness—God would be totally ignored. If you are an overly self-sufficient person, be aware that God may use some other method to get your focus onto Him. But remember that no matter which method He uses to get your attention, it is always an expression of His love.

UNANSWERED PRAYER

The fourth method is sometimes the hardest: God answers even the most fervent prayers by denying our request when our desires are not in sync with His. David implored God to save his infant son's life, but the child died (2 Sam. 12:16–18). It is important to point out that God loves everybody equally, but He has different purposes for each life. The child's death was used to get David's attention in an extreme situation involving the nation's leader who deliberately acted against God's will.

Sin is one reason the Lord will use unanswered prayer to get our attention. Even if the prayer itself is in line with God's will—perhaps even exactly what He wants to do—the Lord may close the doors of heaven and refuse to answer that prayer as a way of forcing us to examine ourselves.

Check the ways you sense God is using to get your attention:

____ **A restless spirit**   ____ **A spoken word**

____ **An unusual blessing**   ____ **Unanswered prayer**

Respond with Samuel's prayer, "Speak, for Your servant is listening" (1 Sam. 3:10, NASB).

How God Gets Our Attention, Part 2

DISAPPOINTMENT

God will sometimes use disappointment to get our attention. In Numbers 14, the nation of Israel was poised at the border of the promised land, ready to take possession of it. However, the "spy committee" voted ten to two against possessing what God promised to give His people in battle. The Scripture describes God's judgment upon the nation for their unbelief. The people acknowledged they had sinned and then changed their minds and desired to enter the land. However, the Lord said no—it was too late. Although there must have been a tremendous sense of disappointment and mourning, God certainly had their attention. It was for their benefit that He revealed the error of not trusting Him. In a similar way, God today allows setbacks to keep us from charting our own course rather than doing His will.

EXTRAORDINARY CIRCUMSTANCES

Sometimes God will use bizarre or unusual circumstances to get us to stop and listen. Moses saw a bush that was on fire but not consumed (Ex. 3:2). As he approached to investigate, the Lord spoke to him from the flame. You and I must learn to look for the presence of God in every circumstance. He leaves His footprints and handiwork all around us, and we will recognize them more often when we are watchful.

Has God used an unusual circumstance to get your attention? _____ If so, describe briefly.

_____

_____

DEFEAT

Another method God uses is defeat. Following the Lord's stunning victory over Jericho, the Israelites approached the small town of Ai with overconfidence, and they neglected to fight in God's strength or with His military plan (Josh. 7). God got Joshua's attention by letting him fail miserably. But notice there is a big difference between failing and being a failure. A terrible defeat may prove to be the greatest stepping-stone to success when we are wise enough to ask, "Lord, what are You saying?"

FINANCIAL TROUBLES

In the Book of Judges, "every man did what was right in his own eyes," and the nation fell into idolatry and disobedience (Judg. 17:6). God brought judgment through the Midianites, who devastated the land, leaving neither livestock nor possessions.

Read Judges 6:3-6 in your Bible. At what point did the Israelites finally cry out to the Lord? _____

God knew exactly what it would take to get their attention. After they turned to Him, He delivered them from their oppressors and blessed them.

TRAGEDY, SICKNESS, AND AFFLICTION

Although we must never look at someone else's situation and presume why God allowed a calamity, we should regard our tragedies and afflictions as reasons to inquire of the Lord, "What are You trying to say?" When King Hezekiah became prideful, God used illness to alert him to the problem (2 Chron. 32:24). Similarly, when Saul of Tarsus was persecuting Christians, he was stricken with blindness—then the Lord certainly had his attention (Acts 9:3–5)!

At any given moment, God knows exactly where you are in your journey and precisely what it will take to get your attention. So be alert; notice if any of God's methods are occurring—or recurring—in your life. Ask Him what He wants to tell you, and then listen, not simply to hear but to obey. Because of His great love for you and His desire to give you a hope and a future, God is always reaching toward you.

Close this study by praying the prayer in the margin.

Prayer:
Father, I surrender my life to You today, knowing that my works will not gain me entrance into the kingdom of God. I trust solely in the blood of Your Son, Jesus Christ, for my strength. Give me a desire for You and for Your Word, and reveal to me the strongholds that prevent me from complete surrender. Amen.

leader Guide

To the Leader:

Each teaching plan provides you with two options for opening the session. Not everyone is ready or able to jump right into a deep discussion of the Bible. So use one of these ideas or create your own idea to begin the session in a way that helps learners feel capable of interacting and sparks their interest in what you are going to discuss.

Before the Session

1. Make and display posters with the words: *Masterpiece, Extraordinary, Exceptional, Remarkable, Work of Art.* [For Step 1 Option]
2. Obtain a piece of fruit—such as an apple, orange, or grapes. [For Step 4]

During the Session

1. Ask: *What is the greatest masterpiece you have ever seen? What made it so extraordinary to you?* OR Draw attention to the displayed posters and ask what the words are used to describe. FOR EITHER OPTION: Ask participants if they consider themselves extraordinary masterpieces and why. Allow time for discussion. Declare that God created us to live an extraordinary life. Read Dr. Stanley's definition of an extraordinary life from the Introduction on page 4. Over the next nine weeks you will look at principles from God's Word that empower believers to live the extraordinary life. Now discuss the Introductory activity on page 5.

2. Ask a volunteer to state the first principle of living the extraordinary life by reading the title for Week 1. Ask how many people desire a complete life of fulfillment and how many actually find it. Request participants state from Day 1 the crucial truth people must grasp if they desire a complete life [see the quotation in the margin]. State that many people cannot accept that God's love is unconditional and so they try to earn it. This striving prevents them from living the extraordinary life. Request participants state aloud the first step toward living the extraordinary life. Urge all learners to make certain that they have trusted in Christ alone for salvation. Discuss reasons many people fail to know God [see last few paragraphs of Day 1]. Explore the costs involved in knowing God. Allow volunteers to share how they have discovered that knowing Christ is worth the cost.

3. Ask: *Do you think everyone who has trusted Christ and knows Him personally is experiencing the extraordinary life? Why or why not?* Discuss what athletes do when they go through a dry spell or seem to lose their edge. State that, like athletes, believers need to go back to the basics. Discuss the second activity of Day 2. Ask volunteers to read aloud John 15:4-5

from several Bible translations. [You can print these off at *www.bible-gateway.com.*] State that a fundamental principle of living a complete life is to abide rather than to strive. Display the fruit and ask if participants consider it an extraordinary masterpiece and why. Ask what that fruit did to create itself. Using the lesson material, help learners determine how believers abide in Christ.

4. Ask: *When you abide in Christ, where does Christ abide?* Read the first sentence of Day 3. Request someone read aloud the first quotation in the margin of Day 3. Ask which learners think is the most difficult—loving God or allowing Him to love them, and why. State that understanding who we are can help us accept love from and express love to God. Lead participants to read the Scriptures under *Who Am I?* in the margin of Day 3 and make "I am" statements about themselves. Ask: *How can knowing who you are empower you to live extraordinarily?*

5. State that God doesn't just want us to know who we are, He wants us to know why He created us. Guide participants to read the Scriptures under *Why Am I Here?* and make statements about their purpose. Inquire: *Why can these purposes cause us to feel guilty or unfulfilled instead of extraordinary?* Declare that we must not fall back into performance-driven religion by trying to fulfill God's purposes on our own. Read the second quotation in Day 3's margin. Encourage learners: *Focus on who you are in Christ and on loving and abiding in Him and your God-given purposes will begin to be fulfilled in your life.* Urge adults to remember to abide, not strive.

6. Declare that part of abiding is listening to and obeying God's directions. Complete the first activity of Day 4. Ask what prevents Christians from listening to God's voice. State that God loves us enough that He will keep after us to get our attention and get us back on track. Use Dr. Stanley's comments and the activities in Days 4 and 5 to discuss the nine ways God gets our attention. Determine what believers must do when they sense God is working to get their attention. Ask: *Why does God even bother to get our attention? Why does He want our complete surrender?* Allow time for discussion.

7. Urge participants to pray silently the closing prayer in Day 5 as you pray it aloud.

God's Grace Is the Starting Point

Secure In My Father's Love

I want to share with you a life-changing experience I had about twenty years ago. I was in my late forties and working hard as a pastor, but I knew something was lacking in my walk with the Lord. I began searching my heart to see if anything was hindering my relationship with God, but I was left with only the keen awareness of the void in my heart.

When this tension in my spiritual life came to a head, I called four of my closest friends. They agreed to meet with me and help me discover what was missing so I could find peace with God. The first night of our meeting, I talked for more than eight hours, telling them everything about myself. Later, I sat up most of the night filling seventeen legal-sized pages with more intimate details of my life.

The following morning I revealed every piece of personal information to my friends. After the group reflected on what I had said, one member asked me to elaborate on the death of my father, who had died when I was nine months old. After I finished, he told me to close my eyes. Then he said, "Picture this: Your father has just picked you up in his arms and is holding you. What do you feel?"

Close your eyes and imagine your Heavenly Father holding you in His arms. What do you feel?

_____

_____

That meeting with my friends took place decades ago, but I remember it vividly. I cried. I felt warm, loved, and secure. I had never felt the amazing depth of my Heavenly Father's love until then. I was saved at twelve years of age, but that meeting with my friends was the first time I felt with all my heart that God truly loved me—not as a distant, impersonal deity, but as my loving, Heavenly Father.

Accepting the incredibly expansive love of God is not easy. For years I was convinced that the distance I felt from God must be linked to some sin in my life. I prayed incessantly for forgiveness, even trying to find sins that weren't there. Many Christians live this way, harboring feelings of shame and self-doubt that have more to do with their fear of intimacy than with reality.

Many people know they are saved but have never discovered the true joy and contentment of being children of God. One of the primary reasons Paul wrote to the believers in Colossae was to express the freedom that was available through Jesus Christ. False teachers had entered their fellowship and taught that while it was right to accept Jesus as the Messiah, one must also live under the regulations of the Mosaic Law.

> "We cannot attest to God's work of grace while living under the bondage of the law."
> —Charles Stanley

The burden was too great for the young church; its people lost their joy and fell into various forms of bondage. People today fall into the same trap when they attempt to demonstrate their Christianity through submission to human rules rather than allegiance to God alone. This is not the way of freedom in Christ. We cannot attest to God's work of grace while living under the bondage of the law. Completeness is found only in Jesus, not in abiding by prescribed rules or regulations.

Read Colossians 2:8-10, printed in the margin. Underline what you must do to maintain your freedom in Christ. Circle what empowers you to be free and content in Christ.

> "See to it that no one takes you captive through philosophy and empty deception, according to the tradition of men, according to the elementary principles of the world, rather than according to Christ. For in Him all the fullness of Deity dwells in bodily form, and in Him you have been made complete" (Col. 2:8-10, NASB).

A New Spirit, A New Life

When we accept Jesus as our Savior, we are given a new spirit—one empowered by the Holy Spirit. Paul told us, "If anyone is in Christ, he is a new creature; the old things passed away; behold, new things have come" (2 Cor. 5:17).

Christ's dwelling within us makes us sufficient and adequate for all things. God has regenerated our spirits. We are partakers of His divine nature, and it is no longer our nature to sin.

"For by these He has granted to us His precious and magnificent promises, so that by them you may become partakers of the divine nature" (2 Pet. 1:4, NASB)

This does not mean that we are perfect or will never sin again; it does not mean that when we abide in close fellowship with Christ, sin loses its appeal. Even though we are new creatures spiritually, our bodies are unchanged. God has given us certain natural appetites that are both normal and essential. Often, when we try to satisfy these appetites in our own strength, we yield to sinful desires. God wants us to understand our position as believers—we are totally complete in the Lord, who has promised to meet all of our needs within His perfect timing.

When we ask Jesus Christ to come into our lives, He will. This is both wonderful and challenging. Yet there still remains a struggle. We have a new nature that no longer corresponds with our old way of doing things. A conflict erupts between serving God and yielding to the desires of the flesh.

In order to triumph over the flesh, you must understand your true identity in Christ. If you begin your Christian walk by thinking that you still have an old sin nature, plan to battle temptation the rest of your life. Sin is easier to yield to when we think we cannot help what we do or feel. We begin to tell ourselves it is just our old carnal nature coming through. Likewise, if you believe that God merely patched you up at the point of salvation, you will spend the rest of your life dealing with discouragement, doubt, and defeat.

With this mentality, we miss the radical truth of salvation; we overlook the truth of God's power in our lives. The moment you are saved, your sin nature dies and Jesus Christ abides in you. You have a new nature in Christ—one of obedience, submission, love, loyalty, and devotion to God. We are new creatures in Him, not partially but completely.

Read Romans 6: 4,11 in your Bible. If you have been baptized as a believer in Jesus Christ, what did you declare with that baptism?

I am _____ to sin, but _____ in Christ.

Paul told us that the old things have passed away. All things are now new. That includes our spirits, our natures, our lives—every part of us. Many of us have a hard time accepting this truth. Often it is more natural to harbor guilt about past wrongs, but God says He has forgiven us of our transgressions and canceled our certificate of debt (Col. 2:13). Christ has canceled all judgment against us as well as condemnation of sin. They were nailed to the cross at Calvary. We no longer have a sin-debt. We don't have to pay the price for our sins. Jesus paid it in full once and for all. Not only did God cancel our sin, He took it away—erased it through the sacrificial death of Jesus Christ. That is why the apostle Peter wrote, "He Himself bore our sins in His body on the cross, so that we might die to sin and live to righteousness" (1 Pet. 2:24).

> "The Christian life is an expression of God's grace rather than a checklist of dos and don'ts."
> —Charles Stanley

We have a new nature, a new sense of liberty, a new freedom in His forgiveness. We have a new standard of conduct that we can keep through the power of the Holy Spirit. All you have to do to experience the extraordinary life is to begin making withdrawals by faith.

The Christian life is an expression of God's grace rather than a checklist of dos and don'ts. What Christianity is all about is the freedom to enjoy the life God has given us, and freedom to share this truth with others.

Read Romans 5:1-2 in your Bible. If you have placed your faith in Christ:

Where do you stand? _____

What do you have as a result?_____

Eternal Security Matters

Many people who trust Christ as their Savior know they are saved but are not quite certain about eternal security, the work of God that assures salvation is permanent. They believe salvation can somehow be lost through wrong actions or a voluntary choice to forfeit it.

Does it really matter if we believe in eternal security? The answer is yes! Eternity is one of God's promises, and He wants His children to be confident about their guaranteed future with Him.

Read 1 John 5:13 in your Bible. Circle the word below that best completes the statement.

John wrote to believers so they could *hope* *think* *pretend* *know* **they had eternal life.**

The Bible teaches that when we receive Jesus Christ as Savior, we unequivocally *have* eternal life. This God-given assurance influences every aspect of our faith. Eternal security is a foundational cornerstone for effective and godly service in the power of the Holy Spirit. A believer who is sure of eternity is not working to get something from God, but is diligently serving Him out of devotion.

Our assurance of salvation depends upon eternal security. If salvation is based upon *anything* other than the completed work of Jesus Christ on the cross, then we find ourselves on shaky ground. Some believers attempt to involve themselves in the salvation process by good works or right behavior; such people are prone to doubts about eternity because they feel they must *earn* God's goodwill and heaven.

Read Ephesians 2:8-9, printed in the margin. Why can we not earn salvation and eternity in heaven?

"For by grace you have been saved through faith; and that not of yourselves, it is the gift of God; not as a result of works, so that no one may boast" (Eph.2:8-9, NASB).

If we add a single work requirement to salvation, then it is no longer a gift; it is payment for services rendered.

We are eternally secure in our Lord. There's not a single verse anywhere in Scripture indicating our salvation lasts only for a season. Notice what the Bible says: the Lord gives believers *eternal* life, and we will *never perish* (John 10:28, emphasis added); we are "*sealed* for the day of redemption" (Eph. 4:30, emphasis added), which means the ultimate day when God calls us home. We are assured that no one can snatch us out of God's hand (John 10:27–30).

Once you've trusted Jesus Christ as your Savior, you may have doubts or fears. You may rebel and sin against Him. But that in no way means you have lost your salvation. If it did imply such a thing, what could God possibly have meant by "I give eternal life to them, and they will *never* perish" (John 10:28, emphasis added)? This isn't license for sin; this is reason to rejoice, to praise God, to walk holy before Him, and to obey Him.

When you and I trusted Jesus as our Savior, we didn't receive just forgiveness of our sins; we received His very life. Through the Holy Spirit, Jesus is right now abiding inside us (John 15:4) to help each believer live the Christian life (Gal. 2:20). He promised that He would not leave us as orphans, fending for ourselves, but instead, He would send us another Helper—the Holy Spirit—who would be with us forever, dwelling not only with us, but in us (John 14:16).

That is a profound difference between believers and unbelievers— both experience life on earth, but we who believe look forward to an abundant life with our Heavenly Father after we die. Jesus was, is, and always will be—He will live forever, and the eternal life He offers is likewise of infinite duration. In addition, He gives us the quality and nature of the life He Himself possesses—it is glorious, abundant, and indescribable. He has given us Himself.

> "My sheep hear My voice, and I know them, and they follow Me; and I give eternal life to them, and they will never perish; and no one will snatch them out of My hand. My Father, who has given them to Me, is greater than all; and no one is able to snatch them out of the Father's hand" (John 10:27-29).

Read John 10:7-10 in your Bible. When can you begin to enjoy Christ's full and eternal life?

Living in Grace

Do you set rules and regulations for your life but then judge yourself very harshly when you do not live up to your expectations? Do you feel close to the Lord when you are doing something religious but distant when you are not? Many people today are living in this manner—they lack assurance that they have pleased God. The Bible says that you and I have been accepted by His grace, which can be defined as God's kindness toward us without consideration of any merit on our part.

In the Old Testament, the ark of the covenant—which symbolized God's presence—was kept in a secured place in the tabernacle called "the holy of holies." Access to this divine place was permitted only once per year and was restricted to the high priest. The Israelite people never were able to get anywhere close to the ark. A personal relationship with God was unthinkable. Instead, their whole concept of relating to God involved living up to laws and achieving acceptance on the basis of performance. The forgiveness of their sin was based on a literal animal sacrifice.

Jesus came to die for our sins and be a permanent, one-time substitutionary sacrifice. Forgiveness was only part of the plan; He came also to initiate an entirely different lifestyle from what the people of God had been experiencing. On the day of Jesus' crucifixion, the veil hiding the ark of the covenant was split from top to bottom, symbolizing that God opened the door to an intimate relationship with Him. He has made it possible for us to talk directly to Him and know we are being heard. That change in relationship reflects the difference between grace and law.

"Therefore, since we have a great high priest who has passed through the heavens, Jesus the Son of God, let us hold fast our confession.... Therefore let us draw near with confidence to the throne of grace, so that we may receive mercy and find grace to help in time of need" (Heb. 4:14,16, NASB).

Read Hebrews 4:14,16, printed in the margin. Underline what is in the holy of holies now that the veil has been split. Circle what you can receive when you go there.

Jesus' death and resurrection settled the basis of our acceptance once and for all. Though our conduct sometimes is not what it ought to be, we are nonetheless embraced as children of God. In order to enjoy the Christian life, we must view ourselves the way God sees us. People trying to live up to an impossible, invisible standard never know when they have pleased God. If life is a matter of rules and regulations, we will never have any peace or contentment.

We have a choice to make. We can set rules and live by legalistic domination, fear, and uncertainty, or we can choose to live in the wonderful acceptance that comes by the cross. The life of grace—lived in His eternal grip—is available to everyone who will call upon Him.

As you read Ephesians 1:3-8 in your Bible, record words used to describe God's grace.

_____

What is the result of this grace? _____

day *Five*

The Transforming Grace of God

God's ultimate will is for every believer to be conformed to the likeness of His Son. His grace is responsible for your rebirth, and from that point it directs, moves, and influences you to become increasingly Christlike.

The apostle Paul's life is a powerful example of God's transforming grace. In Philippians 3, Paul described how he once depended on his good works, nature, and conduct to gain acceptance before God. He did not originally understand there is only one way to be made acceptable in God's sight—by His grace. If good works and religious activity could in some way gain divine approval, Paul never would have written about his former vain attempts to win God's favor and his numerous faulty reasons for confidence (vv. 5–6).

However, encountering the living Christ totally changed Paul, and he explained, "Whatever things were gain to me, those things I have [now] counted as loss" (Phil. 3:7). He recognized that all of his human titles and achievements had absolutely no spiritual value. We too must realize we will never gain eternity by depending on anything we are or anything we do—salvation is unrelated to how much money we give, what excellent citizens we are, or how well we treat our families. It is by grace, and grace alone, that we are saved (Eph. 2:8–9).

"You will not find pride in the heart of a man or a woman who truly understands grace."
—Charles Stanley

There are millions of people who sincerely but wrongly believe they will be acceptable to God based on how good they are. By grace, Paul's thinking was corrected—he learned that everything he had counted as valuable was worthless. In this way, the worst enemy of Christianity became its greatest asset, its greatest motivator, and its dearest friend.

God's grace that saves and transforms today is the same grace that changed Saul, the sinner, into Paul, the apostle.

Once we have been transformed from sinner to saint, four attitudes should become evident. First, we should exhibit true humility.

Read 1 Corinthians 15:9 in your Bible.
How did Paul, the preeminent missionary and preacher of the gospel, describe himself? _____

You will not find pride in the heart of a man or a woman who truly understands grace—that person will always point others to Christ, realizing that anything positive is due entirely to God.

Read 1 Corinthians 15:10. What made Paul what He was? _____

What role has grace played in making you who you are? _____

Paul credited God's grace for his transformation, not anything he did.

The second attitude is one of obligation. Paul was so overwhelmed by the undeserved grace of God that he gave his life to fulfilling the mission the Lord assigned him. He considered it an enormous privilege and gave himself wholeheartedly to the task. The apostle had so much gratitude for his salvation that he had to tell other people what had happened to him. You also have a message to share. Don't be quiet about it. It is wrong to

"For Christ's love compels us, because we are convinced that one died for all"
(2 Cor. 5:14, NIV).

keep God's love to yourself when there is a world of people hurting and dying in agony, sorrow, frustration, anger, disappointment, and despair.

A third thing we should demonstrate is a sense of dependence. Paul mentioned laboring "even more than all of them, yet not I, but the grace of God with me" (1 Cor. 15:10). He was saying that he did not strive through his own efforts; the same grace, goodness, and power that transformed him are the same loving power at work in the believer's life every day. We do not have to depend on our own wisdom, abilities, talents, or strength. It is Christ in us who accomplishes all things (Phil. 4:13), and apart from Him, we can do nothing (John 15:5).

One final attitude we should display is a spirit of absolute confidence. At the end of his life, Paul was able to say, "I have fought the good fight, I have finished the course, I have kept the faith" (2 Tim. 4:7). And Paul looked forward to receiving the crown of righteousness from the Lord Himself (v. 8).

Read 1 Peter 5:10-11,12, printed in the margin. Of what can you be confident because of God's transforming grace? _____

So what can you—and must you—do with the grace of God? _____

> "After you have suffered for a little while, the God of all grace, who called you to His eternal glory in Christ, will Himself perfect, confirm, strengthen and establish you. To Him be dominion forever and ever. Amen....
> I have written to you briefly, exhorting and testifying that this is the true grace of God. Stand firm in it!"
> (1 Pet. 5:10-11,12, NASB).

Paul was an awesome example of the transforming power of God's grace, which took a man murderously opposed to Christ and changed him into the world's greatest missionary. He gave himself without reservation to proclaiming the gospel, and he was able to say that God's grace toward him "did not prove vain" (1 Cor. 15:10). Has God poured His grace into your life? Don't let it be in vain—tell God how thankful you are . . . and tell others why.

Prayer:
Dear Heavenly Father, thank You for the gift of eternal life through the death of Your Son, Jesus Christ. I know that I cannot earn my way into heaven and am not worthy of Your favor—it is a free gift of grace. I pray that You will deepen my desire to know You and teach me the principles of Your Word so I can bring honor and glory to Your name. Amen.

To the Leader:

Meditate on the words to the grand hymn "Grace Greater than Our Sin" (*The Baptist Hymnal* [Nashville: Convention Press, 1991], No. 329).

Consider what role grace has played in making you who you are. How has it transformed you, compelled you? How are you living and standing firm in grace? Class participants will learn far more about grace if they see you living and serving in God's marvelous grace.

During the Session

1. Ask participants to state common phrases that contain the word *grace*. [Samples: Grace period. Grace to you. Say grace before meals. "There but for the grace of God go I."] Discuss how these phrases help (or don't help) learners grasp the meaning or concept of grace. OR Organize participants into small groups. Challenge each group to list as many songs about grace as they can in one minute. [You can distribute hymnals to help groups out.] Allow groups to share their hymn titles. Discuss what those hymns teach us about grace.

2. Invite someone to read aloud the title of Week 2. State that this is the second principle for living the extraordinary life. Declare that we can be secure in God's love because of His grace. Request participants state why they agree or disagree with Dr. Stanley's statement, "Accepting the incredibly expansive love of God is not easy." Discuss why we must accept His love if we want to live the extraordinary life. Explain that Paul wrote to the Colossian Christians who were no longer living the extraordinary life because they had lost their freedom in Christ. Request participants read Colossians 1:3-6 in their Bibles and identify how the Colossians began their walk with Christ. State that although they started out in God's grace, they began to fall into bondage. Ask the class to identify the bondages from Colossians 2:20-22. Request participants to state from Colossians 2:8-10 what Paul told the Colossians to do to maintain their freedom in Christ. Ask them to state phrases from this passage that declare why believers can be free and content in Christ.

3. Ask what we have been given because we are filled with Christ. [See title for Day 2.] Declare that we can be secure in our new nature because of God's grace. Request someone to read aloud 2 Peter 1:4 from the margin of Day 2. Use Dr. Stanley's comments to determine what it does and does not mean to have a new nature. Follow up with: *We all know the conflict between serving God and yielding to our sinful desires, how can we win over our flesh?* Discuss the first activity of Day 2. Evaluate how that position in Christ is strong evidence of His grace. Ask: *What about when we don't act dead to sin and really mess up? How is God's*

grace evident then? Read aloud Romans 5:20-21. Remind participants that God's grace is greater than their sin. Complete the final activity of Day 2. Request participants stand up. Ask: *How does where you stand— in a room, on the street, at a ballgame—determine what you experience at that point in time?* [what they see, what might happen to them, who they relate with, etc.] *How does standing in grace determine what you experience in life?* Explore how believers stand in grace. Allow time for suggestions and discussion.

4. Declare that we are secure for eternity because of God's grace. Ask: *Does it really matter if we believe in eternal security? Why or why not?* Lead the class to contrast the behavior of secure and insecure children. Explore how that translates to believers who are secure or insecure about their eternal future. Ask if participants know people who think they must earn God's good will and heaven. Inquire: *What happens when they do wrong things or don't do enough of the right things?* Discuss the second activity of Day 3. Request someone read aloud from the margin John 10:27-29. Declare that assurance should give us the courage to live an extraordinary life. Discuss the final activity of Day 3.

5. Affirm that since we can enjoy a full and eternal life now, we must live in God's grace. Request participants silently consider their responses as you read Dr. Stanley's opening questions to Day 4. Examine why we can be assured of God's kindness and acceptance regardless of what we have or have not done. Discuss the two activities in Day 4. Ask: *To whom is the kind of life described in Ephesians 1:3-8 available?*

6. State that accepting and living in God's grace transforms us. Briefly describe from Philippians 3 Paul's description of his transformation. Ask the class to state the four attitudes that become evident when we are transformed by grace. Discuss the questions related to 1 Corinthians 15:9-10.

7. Read aloud 1 Peter 5:10-12 as a closing challenge to the class to stand firm in grace. Invite a volunteer to pray the closing prayer from Day 5.

True Effectiveness Comes Through Intimacy With God

day One

A Passion to Know God

Do you have a strong, intense, overwhelming desire to know God? Are your thoughts of Him sweeping and grand, or is your relationship with Him superficial and shallow?

There's quite a difference between *knowing about God* and *knowing God.* Far too many people know about God but do not have a progressively deeper and intimate relationship with Him. More than anything else our Father in heaven wants an intimate relationship with His children.

The prophet Hosea wrote, "Let us know, let us press on to know the LORD. His going forth is as certain as the dawn; and He will come to us like the rain, like the spring rain watering the earth" (Hos. 6:3). God's promises are sure. If we set our hearts and minds to know Him, He will open our spiritual eyes and ears, revealing Himself in wonderful and often unexpected ways.

Spiritual intimacy requires quiet moments when God can speak clearly to your heart and when you can speak honestly to Him. We need to spend time alone in prayer, meditation, and worship.

We also must give ourselves to the study of the Scriptures. The Bible reveals who God is and what He has done. If we really want to know Him, we will set aside time to partake of the living Word, letting His divine counsel saturate our minds. Reading spiritual biographies of godly people can further augment our walk with God as we observe how He has worked in their lives. They have a great deal to tell us about God's ways.

Read Psalm 42:1-2 and Jeremiah 29:12-13 in your Bible. Then describe in the margin essential actions and attitudes for nurturing an intimate relationship with God.

day Two

Knowing God as Your Father

When you pray, by what name do you address God?

_____

While all of the grandiose titles we have given Him are appropriate, we Christians have the awesome privilege of calling God "Father." We can also *know* Him that way.

The possibility of having a personal relationship with God was a revolutionary concept before Christ lived as a human (Matt. 6:9). The Old Testament contains only fifteen references to God as "Father," and those speak primarily of Him as the Father of the Hebrew people; the idea of Him being a personal God to individuals is not evident until the New Testament. Yet that is the reason Jesus Christ came to earth— to die on the cross for our sins and reveal the Heavenly Father so you and I might know Him intimately.

"Father," which appears 245 times in the New Testament, was Jesus' favorite terminology for God—He spoke it more than ten times just in the Sermon on the Mount (Matt. 5–7), and He also used the name to begin the prayer. The Lord's purpose was to reveal that God is not merely a transcendent force somewhere in the universe but a loving, personal, Heavenly Father who is profoundly interested in the details of our lives.

The privilege of knowing God as Father involves more than acquaintance with Him as a person or Spirit; it goes beyond simple familiarity with His matchless grace, love, and kindness, and even surpasses

> "God is not merely a transcendent force somewhere in the universe but a loving, personal, Heavenly Father who is profoundly interested in the details of our lives."—Charles Stanley

knowing Him in His holiness, righteousness, and justice. How wonderful that we—mere creations—are able to know God personally as our very own heavenly parent. By addressing Him as "Father," Jesus revealed His intention that we understand what the Old Testament saints could not fully grasp—we can have the blessing of intimate kinship with the living God of the universe.

What indications of intimacy do you observe in Romans 8:14-17?

In fact, it is through the person of Jesus Christ that we are able to know God in this way. Unfortunately, many people mistakenly think that such privilege belongs to all humanity. We sometimes hear phrases such as "fatherhood of God" and "brotherhood of man"; these official-sounding terms express the faulty idea that God is everybody's Father and we are everybody's brother. Of course, since God is the Creator of life, we could in one sense identify Him as the Father of mankind. But the Bible uses the name "Father" to indicate a close, personal relationship, which certainly is not true of all humanity.

day *Three*

How God Expresses His Fatherhood

By observing God's fathering pattern, we can better understand our relationship with Him. And by following His lead, we will be able to express parenthood properly to our own children. With that in mind, notice these seven aspects of God's Fatherhood to us.

HE DESIRES AN INTIMATE RELATIONSHIP WITH US

The Bible tells us to address Him as "Father," and not just as "God," "King," "Holy One," or "Judge." While we should know Him in all these ways, He wants us to realize we can and should approach Him openly and transparently about everything, including needs, weaknesses, and failures.

Read John 6:37 in your Bible. What does God promise those who approach Him?

_____

GOD LONGS TO COMMUNICATE WITH US

Matthew 6:6 tells us to find a secluded place and pray to our Father, "who sees what is done in secret [and] will reward" us. In other words, He hears when we speak to Him, and He answers prayer. He is the kind of Father we can talk to, and though He may not give us everything we want, He will respond to our requests by giving what He knows is best for us (Matt. 7:7–11).

GOD LOVES EACH OF US UNCONDITIONALLY

It is God's nature to love both saint and sinner, based exclusively on the fact that He *is* love (1 John 4:8). The unbeliever has simply positioned himself in such a way that he cannot experience that love—a situation that can be remedied by trusting Jesus as Savior.

OUR HEAVENLY FATHER MEETS ALL OUR NEEDS

Scripture assures us that God knows our needs, even before we ask Him, and He will supply them all "according to His riches in glory in Christ Jesus" (Matt. 6:8; Phil. 4:19). His resources are limitless, so we can be certain no need will go unmet.

Read Matthew 10:29-31 in your Bible. Why will God meet all your needs?

_____

"But you, when you pray, go into your inner room, close your door and pray to your Father who is in secret, and your Father who sees what is done in secret will reward you. And when you are praying, do not use meaningless repetition as the Gentiles do, for they suppose that they will be heard for their many words. So do not be like them; for your Father knows what you need before you ask Him. Pray, then, in this way: 'Our Father who is in heaven, Hallowed be Your name '" (Matt. 6:6-9, NASB).

GOD DISCIPLINES HIS CHILDREN

He trains us not out of anger but with loving correction for our own good. This training is evidence that we are truly His children (Heb. 12:5–10).

GOD ALWAYS GUIDES US TO DO WHAT IS RIGHT

Jesus said the Holy Spirit—our Counselor—would guide us into all truth (John 14:26; 16:13). God never leads us in the wrong direction; He will make our "paths straight" if we trust Him instead of our own intuition (Prov. 3:5–6).

OUR HEAVENLY FATHER IS ALWAYS WITH US

While human parents cannot guarantee they will physically be with their children forever, what does God promise in Hebrews 13:5?

_____

God's Spirit, which dwells within us, is always available to guide and to prompt us.

day *Four*

Why God Speaks

Read Hebrews 1:1-2. What did God do in the past that He still continues to do today?

_____

The God we serve is not a distant, silent deity. You might wonder, *Why would God want to communicate today? What does He have to say to us?*

I believe there are several reasons God speaks. The first is that He loves us and desires an intimate bond with His children. As with any growing relationship, conversation has to flow in two directions: We must be willing not only to talk to Him, but also to listen to Him.

A second reason is to give us guidance. God's people today need as much wisdom and counsel as did the saints of the Bible—we still require direction regarding finances, family, career, church, health, and daily life. Divine wisdom is essential if we are to make sound decisions. This is the reason God sent the Holy Spirit to be our guide and teacher (John 16:13; 14:26). One way the Spirit works is by "illumination"—this happens when we are reading God's Word and suddenly His message to us becomes clear. If we want the Spirit to illuminate the deep truths of the Lord, we've got to give Him something to work with. We must regularly take in words of Scripture so He can help us understand their meaning.

Another reason for His speaking is to bring us comfort and assurance. In Scripture, God spoke to numerous people undergoing hardships and persecution; reminding them of His sovereign control over their situations fortified their faith. We are no different from the people of Bible times—just as the children of Israel needed God's confidence to cross the Red Sea, you and I go through turbulent experiences in our lives, and our faith also needs to be strengthened.

**Read 2 Thessalonians 2:16-17, printed in the margin.
What kind of comfort and hope does God give?**

_____

_____

A final reason—and, I believe, the primary one—is that God wants us to know Him. Though we can never fully grasp all the facets and wonders of who God is, He wants us to spend our lives discovering more and more about Him. He speaks to you, His child, to reveal more of His limitless qualities.

"Now may our Lord Jesus Christ Himself and God our Father, who has loved us and given us eternal comfort and good hope by grace, comfort and strengthen your hearts in every good work and word" (2 Thess. 2:16-17, NASB).

Our Father's Voice

God uses a number of methods to communicate with us: He speaks through His Word and the Holy Spirit as well as through people and circumstances. God has specific purposes for imparting His thoughts to us. He desires that we comprehend His truth so it can shape our lives and so we can share His good news with others.

If God has a particular intention for communicating with us, we have to ask, "What happens when we fail to listen?" We can find the answer at the beginning of the Bible, in the account of Adam and Eve. By studying the account in Genesis 3, we can identify eight consequences of ignoring the Lord's instructions.

Take a few minutes to read carefully Genesis 3:1-19 in your Bible.

1. WE END UP LISTENING TO THE WRONG VOICES (GEN. 3:1–2)

Eve had unmistakably heard God's command. But even having understood, she began to listen to another voice. The serpent spoke and inserted a question mark into her recollection of God's words: "Indeed, has God said . . . ?" The woman allowed herself to be drawn into conversation with him. The voice she listened to was unfamiliar—it was the voice of neither her Creator nor her husband, yet she paid attention and allowed it to supplant God's clear instruction. As a result, she fell into sin—just like anyone today who stops listening to God and offers an ear to Satan.

Consider how many voices we hear in a given day. What we read and hear continually bombards our minds, hearts, and spirits. Between the television, the radio, the newspaper, and magazines—not to mention the opinions of friends and coworkers—we are barraged with vain, erroneous, ungodly philosophy. We must choose whether or not to listen to it. When we fail to heed God's words or to continually remind ourselves of scriptural principles, we begin to listen to wrong voices, and then we drift away from God.

2. WE ARE EASILY DECEIVED (GEN. 3:4)

Notice how Satan took what God said and distorted it. The Lord told Adam and Eve that if they ate from the tree of the knowledge of good and evil, they would "surely die" (Gen. 2:17). Satan used just enough truth to sound credible, but then embellished ever so slightly: "You surely will not die!" It is Satan's nature to lie and deceive, "because there is no truth in him . . . he is a liar and the father of lies" (John 8:44).

Satan deceives with what he knows will appeal, not the truth. He says, "You need this," "You ought to have that," or "This is exactly what you have been looking for." He probably said, "Now, Eve, you need to get the full picture: God doesn't want you to know what He knows, because the day you eat of that tree's fruit, you are going to be just like God." It so happens that Eve did learn some things when she partook. How many of us have learned some things we wish we never knew?

3. WE YIELD TO PRIDE AND INDEPENDENCE (PROV. 16:17–19)

The ultimate root of all sin is pride—it is the equivalent of our saying that we know better than God and can handle the situation our own way.

This is in reality an act of rebellion because it is impossible to know better than an omniscient, all-wise God. His commands are not given to make life dull; every single "thou shalt not" in the Bible is an expression of His love and protection for His children.

4. WE MAKE DECISIONS THAT APPEAL TO THE FLESH (GEN. 3:6)

Satan never tempts us by offering spiritual growth, improved prayer life, or more effective ways to share our faith. No, Satan always appeals to the flesh, not to the spirit. There is nothing wrong with God-given desires, but Satan takes our legitimate longings and, with our cooperation, gets them out of balance. As he did with Eve, the Devil appeals to three yearnings we all have—human appetites, beauty, and wisdom. Then he twists them so that instead of simply desiring and enjoying them, we begin to lust after them and be controlled by them. So, what God gave in freedom ends up enslaving us. By relying on the Holy Spirit, however, we can have

"The highway of the upright is to depart from evil; He who watches his way preserves his life. Pride goes before destruction, and a haughty spirit before stumbling. It is better to be humble in spirit with the lowly than to divide the spoil with the proud" (Prov. 16:17-19, NASB).

the wisdom and direction to keep yearnings within the parameters God designed for us.

5. WE EXCUSE OUR WRONGS AND BLAME OTHERS (GEN. 3:12–13)

When God asked Adam why he was hiding, he immediately pointed at Eve. In fact, there is even a sense of his blaming God for having given him the woman! In turn, Eve blamed the serpent. Neither one could rightly pass the blame because both knew the command and were therefore responsible. Besides, the Devil can't make a believer do anything; we may consent to give in to his temptation, but we are ultimately accountable for that decision. People today blame everyone from parents and coworkers to society itself. But we must recognize that passing the buck doesn't solve anything and that we are responsible before God for our choices and behavior.

6. WE SUFFER THE CONSEQUENCES (GEN. 3:14–19)

All three parties involved had to face the results of their disobedience. Satan was sentenced to eventual destruction. Next, God announced that woman would be ruled by man and would experience pain in childbirth. He also declared that man would have to leave the garden and toil laboriously to earn a living. Furthermore, humans would ultimately experience death.

7. WE CAUSE OTHERS AROUND US TO SUFFER (GEN. 3:6,17–19)

We have seen how sin and its resulting misery extended from the first woman to the first man when she gave him the forbidden fruit. Anguish continued to spread as sin further poisoned their family: The Bible records that Adam and Eve's firstborn son, Cain, murdered his younger brother, Abel. In the earth's very first family, we witness murder, jealousy, and strife. Down through the centuries, Satan has in one way or another had his impact of discord, turmoil, or bloodshed in all families. Everyone is affected because sin is not something that we can isolate. In other words, if you and I sin against God, we are going to hurt somebody else.

8. WE MISS OUT ON GOD'S BEST

When God created Adam and Eve, He intended for them to live in the garden of Eden with all of its absolute perfection. There, God had

"Therefore the LORD God sent him out from the garden of Eden, to cultivate the ground from which he was taken. So He drove the man out; and at the east of the garden of Eden He stationed the cherubim and the flaming sword which turned every direction to guard the way to the tree of life" (Gen. 3:23-24, NASB).

provided for their every possible need, and in addition, they felt no guilt or shame (Gen. 2:25). Yet they chose to disobey, and as a result, the first family suffered horrible consequences, including being cast out of their flawless environment.

How can you resist the lure of competing voices that cause such terrible consequences? (Hint: See John 17:21.)

_____

_____

There is no substitute for personal intimacy with God. Nothing compares with it—it is the key to everything. Most people are looking for an exciting and fulfilling life, and they're looking in all the wrong places: money, prestige, and relationships—mostly relationships. They are looking for something that they can achieve to bring about fulfillment or for someone they can meet who will make their small life grow. But there isn't anything we can do or anyone we can meet who will sufficiently fill the void in our hearts. As Thomas Aquinas said, "There is a God-shaped void in all of us." The only thing that can fill the indescribable longing within each human heart is God's presence. The gift of His Son abiding in us is totally adequate for everything we do.

In order to experience intimacy with the Heavenly Father, you must genuinely regard Him as more important than everything else you pursue in life. It is important to have goals and relationships, but your primary pursuit should be to know God, and to know Him intimately.

Prayer:

Dear Heavenly Father, I know that I cannot manufacture a desire to love You as deeply as I ought. I pray that You will place in my heart a hunger for Your Word and a longing for fellowship with You. Amen.

If God has spoken to you in this lesson and you desire resources for further study, the following are available at *www.lifeway.com* online catalog: *Knowing the Heart of the Father* by David Eckman; *Forty Days on the Mountain: Meditations on Knowing God* by Stephen Smallman; and *Discerning the Voice of God* by Priscilla Shirer.

leader Guide

NOTES

Before the Session

To the Leader:

Consider how well you really know your class participants. Make an effort to deepen your relationship with at least one learner this week. During your interaction with that adult, find a way to share your own passion for knowing God.

For each participant, prepare a worksheet on which you have listed, "Work, Hobbies, Family, Possessions, Friends." [For Step 1 Option]

During the Session

1. Ask: *What's the correlation between leading a full, meaningful life and enjoying close relationships with other people? Why?* OR Distribute the worksheets you prepared earlier. Request participants rank from 1-5 the influence each category has on making their lives full and meaningful, with 1 having the greatest influence and 5 the least. Allow time for participants to complete their assignment. Ask volunteers to share their rankings. Discuss the question asked above.

2. State that if intimacy with others provides times of fulfillment, then we can certainly understand the third principle of living the extraordinary life. Request someone read aloud the title for Week 3. Invite a volunteer to read aloud Hosea 6:3. Evaluate the difference between *knowing God* and *knowing about God*. Ask what it takes to develop and maintain close relationships, especially for busy adults. Discuss the activity for Day 1. Point out that Jeremiah 29:12-13 follows the well-loved verse 11; read that verse. Ask: *How does the context of these three verses together help you further grasp the relationship between this third principle and living the extraordinary life?* Discuss ways adults can seek God with all their hearts.

3. Ask the first question from Day 2. Encourage participants to give reasons for their answers. Explore why knowing God as Father contributes to a greater intimacy with Him. Discuss the last activity of Day 2. Request someone read aloud Matthew 6:9. Ask: *Who can truly call God Father?* [those who honor His name] State that many people hold to the concept that God is everybody's personal Father. Instruct participants to listen for reasons this concept is faulty as volunteers read aloud John 8:19; 10:30; 14:7; and 15:23. Call for responses. Discuss why having an "intimate kinship with the living God of the universe" would naturally result in extraordinary living.

4. Guide the class to state qualities and actions of a good father. Record responses on a writing surface. Request a volunteer read aloud Matthew 7:9-11. Ask: *What are good gifts God gives us?* Use Dr. Stanley's comments and the activities in Day 3 to discuss the seven aspects of God's Fatherhood and compare them to the list you made regarding earthly fathers. [If most of your participants have children, discuss how they can be better parents by emulating God's expressions of fatherhood.]

5. Complete the first activity of Day 4. Organize the class into several small groups. Instruct each group to list reasons they talk to people, and then compare their lists with the reasons enumerated in Day 4 that God speaks. Ask them to consider: *Are your reasons and God's reasons to speak the same or different? Would you add more reasons God speaks to this discussion? If so, what are they?* Allow groups to share what they discussed. Invite someone to read aloud 2 Thessalonians 2:16-17 from the margin on page 35. Invite volunteers to share ways God has comforted them. Encourage them to share Scriptures that have particularly given them eternal comfort, good hope, and strength.

6. Request the class state methods God uses to communicate with His children. Encourage participants to share how God most often speaks to them or an unusual way God has spoken to them. Ask: *Why does God share His thoughts with us?* Then ask: *Do we always listen? Why or why not?* State that Genesis 3 identifies eight consequences of not listening when the Father speaks. Request two or three volunteers read aloud Genesis 3:1-19. Use Dr. Stanley's remarks in Day 5 to discuss the eight consequences. Invite participants to share (without giving specifics or names) how they have personally experienced or observed these consequences. Discuss the final activity of Day 5. Guide participants to reword the eight consequences listed in Day 5 to reflect positively what happens in believers' lives when they choose to be united with the Father in personal intimacy.

7. Ask: *Why are the human relationships we listed earlier not enough for us to live the extraordinary life?* Discuss how believers can achieve the intimacy with God that Jesus prayed for us in John 17:21. Encourage participants to spend a few moments in quiet prayer, expressing their desire to have an intimate relationship with Him. Close by praying the prayer at the conclusion of Day 5.

Trust the Lord

day One

Can You Trust God?

When things are going your way, trusting the Lord is easy. But when painful trials come into your life, leaving you frustrated, anxious, or despairing, do you trust Him then? In the face of adversity, many people wonder, *Does God really love me?* and they conclude that a truly caring Father would not allow sorrow and difficulty to touch His children's lives. Oftentimes they start to question whether God is even *willing* to do anything about their circumstances.

Read Psalm 50:15 in your Bible. What does God assure His people?

_____

Even when we cannot understand why God would allow certain situations to occur, there are *three essential truths* that form the basis for trusting Him, no matter what.

GOD IS PERFECT IN HIS LOVE

God *always* does what is best for us. If we really believe this, we will trust Him even in our most difficult trials. Satan, who works to undermine our trust, often takes advantage of adversity by calling the Father's motives into question. He whispers, "If the Lord really loved you, He would not have allowed this to happen"—he wants us to associate the sting of spiritual discipline with a lack of divine caring. However, the exact opposite is true. Hebrews 12:6 tells us, "Those whom the Lord loves He disciplines, and He scourges every son whom He receives." So, while natural thinking says peace and happiness are tokens of God's love, the Bible says difficulty and discipline are actually evidence of our membership in His family. The reason is clear: God cares for us so much that He will not allow us to stay as we are. Instead, He wants to transform us into the likeness of His Son.

We *can* depend on God's love because of His *character*—it is His very nature to love (1 John 4:8). He could never mistreat one of His children. He will always do what is positive and caring in our lives. *Calvary* is indisputable evidence of God's sacrificial, infinite love for humanity (Rom. 5:8).

"But God demonstrates His own love toward us, in that while we were yet sinners, Christ died for us" (Rom. 5:8, NASB).

GOD IS INFINITE IN WISDOM

God never has to poll the angelic host—or anyone else—to get a consensus about the wisest action to take. In His unlimited knowledge, He always knows what is in our very best interests and acts accordingly. Regardless of what our circumstances look like, we must remember that God knows the optimal course of action in every situation and will only benefit His children.

"Great is our Lord and abundant in strength; His understanding is infinite" (Ps. 147:5, NASB).

Sometimes we look at difficulties facing us and think, *Well now, Lord, I know You are infinitely wise, but I think You've forgotten something.* Be assured He has not overlooked a single factor. In our limited understanding and reasoning, we simply do not see things from God's perspective. We may have all the information that is humanly possible to gather, but God is aware of *everything* influencing the situation as well as all the potential consequences for you and others. He alone comprehends the totality of every single decision. And because He is infinitely wise, He simply cannot make a mistake (Prov. 3:5–6).

However, while God completely understands every situation, He is under no obligation whatsoever to inform us of the rationale for His actions or decisions.

Read 1 Corinthians 1:20,25 in your Bible and fill in the blanks:

Man's greatest wisdom is _____ while

God's "foolishness" is _____.

GOD IS COMPLETELY SOVEREIGN IN HIS CONTROL

Because He *is* sovereign He has perfect, complete control over every last detail of life.

Read John 19:10-11 in your Bible.

What did Pilate assume? _____

How did the Lord set Pilate straight? _____

Earlier, Jesus reassured His disciples that not even a common sparrow—worth only half a penny—could fall to the ground apart from the Father's will (Matt. 10:29). In other words, whether the circumstance is large or small, God is in absolute control.

Some might ask, "Then what about plane crashes or fires or terrorist attacks? Where is God in all that?"

I always go back to Psalm 103:19: "The LORD has established His throne in the heavens, and His sovereignty rules over all." I don't know why God allowed the Holocaust to occur. I don't know why thousands of people died at the hands of terrorists on September 11, 2001. Or why a tsunami killed more than 170,000 people in some of the poorest countries on the face of the earth.

We live in a wicked, vile world where we are subject to the consequences of sin. Many circumstances are not God's perfect will, but He allows them through His permissive will, despite the pain they cause. In His omniscience, God knows what is ultimately best, including the long-term consequences of tragedies that seem heartless and inexplicable. We should not doubt God or abandon our trust when we lack understanding. Instead, we should surrender our lives to Him, accepting by faith that He is good and worthy of our full trust.

So when you face struggles, remind yourself that God has your best interest in mind. He wants you to trust Him. There is no reason to doubt Him, because He is perfect in His love, infinite in His wisdom, and sovereign in His control of the entire universe. Why should believers ever fret, when even in the deepest, darkest valleys there can be abiding joy and confidence? No matter what befalls you, our all-loving, all-wise, all-powerful Heavenly Father has you in the cradle of His hand.

Walking By Faith

Colossians 2:6 gives us an important command: "As you have received Christ Jesus the Lord, so walk in Him."

How did you and I receive Christ? _____

In order to be born again, we trusted the testimony of God's Word. The Christian life is to be "walked"—or lived out—in the same way. By faith.

Many people walk by sight and feelings, but allowing our physical senses to guide us spiritually does not work because the Lord simply will not provide all the information we would like to have. Instead, He wants us to trust Him daily for whatever need we may have. That is why followers of Jesus Christ are commanded to "walk by faith, not by sight" (2 Cor. 5:7). Walking by faith means having a personal relationship with Jesus Christ that results in trusting Him for every circumstance and believing He will do what is right and what benefits us every time, without exception.

According to Hebrews 11:6, printed in the margin, the two essentials to living a faith-motivated life are believing:

1. _____

2. _____

Positively rewrite Hebrews 11:6a to reflect the rewarding result of walking by faith.

With _____ it is possible to _____ _____.

"And without faith it is impossible to please Him, for he who comes to God must believe that He is and that He is a rewarder of those who seek Him" (Heb. 11:6, NASB).

day Three

What Does It Take to Live a Life of Faith?

A DESIRE TO KNOW GOD AND TO BE KNOWN BY HIM

God desires to know each of His children intimately. Therefore, if you pray for the desire to know Him, you can be certain that He will fill your heart with longing for Him. A genuine desire for God cannot be manufactured, but it can be easily acquired—all you have to do is ask for it.

A COMMITMENT TO OBEY HIM

Read Hebrews 11:7-8 in your Bible. Noah and Abraham demonstrated faith by _____.

Obedience is a mark of our ability to trust God, especially when it comes to facing important decisions or serious challenges. God may direct us along a certain course, but we sometimes find ourselves doubting His ability to protect and deliver us safely. However, a person who lives by faith will continue moving forward as Abraham did, without yielding to feelings of doubt or fear. God always rewards obedience with great blessing.

A CONFIDENT CONVICTION GOD WILL FULFILL EVERY PROMISE

The ultimate question is not "Will God do what He promised?" but "Am I willing to trust Him even though His timetable may not be mine?"

Read Hebrews 11:13-16 in your Bible. What amazes you about the faith of the people listed in Hebrews 11?

_____

We must realize that the faith demonstrated by Abel, Enoch, Noah, Abraham, Jacob, and Sarah was faith without limits (Heb. 11). Each one of those people trusted God despite the fact that they did not see the end result of their confidence in Him. They lived by faith each day, and God gave them an eternal reward.

A LIFESTYLE OF FAITH

A life of faith is dominated by Jesus Christ, not selfish desires. The person of little faith says, "God can." The person of great faith says, "God will." But the person with perfect faith says, "God has done it."

As you read Hebrews 10:36-39, printed in the margin, underline qualities necessary to lead a lifestyle of faith. Circle the end result of a lifestyle of faith.

Barriers to Faith

Why do we experience barriers to our faith? Like Moses, many people have a limited understanding of God. At first, Moses could not comprehend what God was telling him to do. How could he lead millions out of Egyptian bondage? Afraid that he could not rise to the task to which God called him, Moses presented five reasons to prove his calculations were correct. Perhaps, at some point, you have felt the same way.

1. A POOR SELF-IMAGE

Read Exodus 3:11. What question did Moses ask that reflected his poor self-image? _____

Moses was a shepherd, and Egyptians loathed shepherds. Because he had assessed his life apart from the miraculous work of God, the prophet denied he could be of any use to God. But God takes great joy in doing the impossible through the lives of men and women who place their trust in Him. So remember, what seems impossible for you is an opportunity for God to display His infinite ability.

"For you need endurance, so that after you have done God's will, you may receive what was promised. For in yet a very little while, the Coming One will come and not delay. But My righteous one will live by faith; and if he draws back, My soul has no pleasure in him. But we are not those who draw back and are destroyed, but those who have faith and obtain life" (Heb. 10:36-39, HCSB).

"Then Moses said to God, 'Indeed, when I come to the children of Israel and say to them, "The God of your fathers has sent me to you," and they say to me, "What is His name?" what shall I say to them?' And God said to Moses, 'I AM WHO I AM.' And He said, 'Thus you shall say to the children of Israel, "I AM has sent me to you." ' "
(Ex. 3:13-14, NASB).

2. IGNORANCE OF WHO GOD IS

Moses had heard the name Yahweh, but he did not have a personal knowledge of the God of Israel. However, this changed when he stepped into the presence of the living Lord at the burning bush. That was where God began to develop Moses' spiritual character, a process that continued throughout his life.

3. DOUBT

Read Exodus 4:1. How did Moses express doubt in God? _____

Moses doubted God's ability, and his doubt kept him from experiencing the fullness of God's immediate blessings. Each of us has faced times when we were not sure of God's involvement in our circumstances. We have wondered if we could trust His promises, and we have questioned the Christian principles that we had been applying to our lives.

God never allows us to face a challenge without providing a promise for us to cling to in times of trial and adversity. A lack of trust in God's ability often leads to feelings of unrest and anxiety. Doubt keeps us from accomplishing God's will, but it also prevents us from experiencing His goodness.

Moses did not realize it, but the moment he decided to obey God was the first step he took toward an eternal blessing. How do you experience God's goodness? Lay aside your doubts. Place your trust in the omnipotent potential of an all-knowing God who loves and understands you completely and will never allow you to experience defeat.

4. INADEQUACY

One of Moses' strongest excuses was that he could not speak eloquently. Therefore, he argued, he could not go to the people of Israel with God's message, nor could he go to Pharaoh (Ex. 4:10).

A person who thinks he is of great value to God is deceived. Those who know they need God are the ones most often used by Him to do great work. When we think we are bright, talented, and strong, we usually have little need of God. Our minds are set on what we can accomplish, and we do not seek the wisdom of the Lord. But depending solely on our own strength can lead to feelings of doubt, insecurity, and anxiety.

The person with a humble heart knows that he can do nothing apart from God, and this is his greatest asset. Moses was overwhelmed by his challenge, but God's ability surpassed anything he faced. Whatever your inadequacy, it is an opportunity for God to prove His faithfulness through you.

5. FEAR OF FAILURE

Read Exodus 4:13. How did Moses express his fear of failure? _____

Fear of failure is one of the most debilitating and common fears people suffer from. Many people are actually more afraid to fail than to die. I am convinced that this is why so many people struggle to rest completely in God's grace—they are afraid He will let them fail. But God will never give you a directive and then leave you to work out the details by yourself. Instead, He is personally involved in every aspect of your life.

Which of the barriers to Moses' faith are also barriers to your faith?
❏ **Poor self-image**   ❏ **Ignorance of who God is**
❏ **Doubt**   ❏ **Inadequacy**   ❏ **Fear of failure**

According to Ephesians 3:20-21, printed in the margin, why shouldn't there be any barriers to your living the extraordinary life?

"Now to Him who is able to do far more abundantly beyond all that we ask or think, according to the power that works within us, to Him be the glory in the church and in Christ Jesus to all generations forever and ever. Amen" (Eph. 3:20-21, NASB).

---

day *Five*

The Faith That Conquers

How do you gain a conquering faith? From the story of David and Goliath in 1 Samuel 17 we learn several principles.

Read in your Bible 1 Samuel 17:1-11,31-32. What was Israel's greater enemy? ❑ **Goliath** ❑ **Their fear**
What was Israel's greater asset?
❑ **A powerful king** ❑ **A trusting youth**

RECALL PAST VICTORIES

David recalled how God had delivered him from the paw of the lion and the grasp of the bear (1 Sam. 17:32–37). Spiritual victories are won in your mind. If you give in to feelings of fear, doubt, and unbelief, you will suffer defeat because your mental focus shifts from God and His infinite ability to the lies of the enemy. Set the focus of your heart, mind, and will on the truth of God's Word, and you will gain the victory in every battle.

In the margin, describe how God has given you a victory in the past. How does that give you faith that He will be victorious in your present battle?

REEXAMINE AND REAFFIRM YOUR MOTIVES

David did not rush into battle without assessing the situation. He realized that the battle facing Israel was spiritual in nature and not just physical. His primary motivation for seeking the victory was not personal gain. Instead, it was to bring glory to God.

If your motives for victory are selfish in nature, God will deal with you. True victory and peace can come only as you surrender your life, along with your desires, to Christ. In yielding yourself to Him, you gain a deeper joy and sense of fulfillment. Always ask three questions before dealing with any conflict or challenge: *What is my motivation? What is God's purpose for me?* and *What really is going on here?* Take time to pray and seek God's will for every situation.

REJECT DISCOURAGING WORDS

There was no one to encourage David in his quest to defeat Goliath.

Read 1 Samuel 17:28,33. Describe the response David received from:
His brother _____
King Saul _____

If David had listened to their comments, he would have given up. Instead, he turned his heart toward God, and it was there that he found the encouragement he needed. From a human perspective, there may be times when you feel as though you are facing a Goliath alone. But God has promised never to leave you (Heb. 13:5). His Spirit is with you in every circumstance.

RECOGNIZE THE TRUE NATURE OF THE BATTLE

Goliath cursed David when he saw him.

Read 1 Samuel 17:45-47, printed in the margin. Underline what David recognized was the true nature of the battle.

RESPOND TO THE CHALLENGE WITH A POSITIVE CONFESSION

David made positive confessions of faith to those around him. He asked his critics, "Who is this uncircumcised Philistine, that he should taunt the armies of the living God?" (1 Sam. 17:26). To Saul he said, "The LORD who delivered me . . . will deliver me from the hand of this Philistine" (1 Sam. 17:37). And to Goliath he said, "I come to you in the name of the LORD of hosts, the God of the armies of Israel" (1 Sam. 17:45). David's words were a testimony of faith. He was convinced that he could not lose, because God was with him.

RELY ON THE POWER OF GOD FOR THE VICTORY

David did not need a spear or a javelin to defeat Goliath. He needed only a conquering faith and a willingness to follow God. A homemade slingshot was the weapon God chose for him. Human strength was not the victor. God was the One who received the glory.

RECKON THE VICTORY

Once you have spent time with God in prayer and know it is His will for you to enter the battle, you can reckon the victory to be His. Even before he stepped on the battlefield, David knew he would not lose.

You can face any circumstance with confidence and hope because it is not your strength, wisdom, energy, or power that is the ultimate source of victory. It is God's ability, and when you place your trust in Him, you tap into an eternal force that cannot be harnessed by any human constraints.

"You come to me with a sword, a spear, and a javelin, but I come to you in the name of the LORD of hosts, the God of the armies of Israel, whom you have taunted. This day the LORD will deliver you up into my hands . . . that all the earth may know that there is a God in Israel, and that all this assembly may know that the LORD does not deliver by sword or by spear; for the battle is the LORD's and He will give you into our hands" (1 Sam. 17:45–47)

Prayer:
Dear Heavenly Father, thank You for caring about me enough to send Your Son to atone for my sin. Thank You for knowing when I get up and when I sleep. Thank You for the plan You have for my life. I pray You will help me to trust in You and take my strength from You to slay the giants in my life. Amen.

leader Guide

To the Leader:

Read Romans 4:16-21. Examine your own faith—do you waver in unbelief at God's promise or are you fully convinced that what He has promised He is able to perform? Pray for God to strengthen your trust in Him so you can live the extraordinary life and, by example, exhort your class to do the same.

During the Session

1. Ask participants: *Did you accomplish everything you wanted to this week? Why or why not?* Ask two volunteers to read aloud Psalm 57:1-2 and 138:7-8. Lead the class to discuss how the psalmists expressed a relationship between trusting God and having God's purposes accomplished in their lives. OR Ask participants who have participated in an outdoors community-building exercise to describe how they had to trust others as they fell, jumped, or climbed. Ask: *Did you complete everything or back out? How did you feel? What would you say is the relationship between trust and living extraordinarily?*

2. State that the fourth principle for living the extraordinary life is that when we trust the Lord He will move heaven and earth to accomplish His purpose. Discuss the first activity of Day 1. Ask when participants might find that promise easiest and hardest to believe. Dr. Stanley described three essential truths that express why we can trust God. Ask someone to state the first truth. Consider what Satan tries to convince believers in tough times. Encourage learners to read John 8:44 in their Bibles and state what we know about Satan. Request participants recall a time they disciplined their child(ren) (or were disciplined as a child). Ask: *What was the reason for the discipline? Did your child(ren) like it? Why did you enforce it anyway? Why can God's discipline actually reassure us His love for us is perfect?*

3. Ask if participants have ever been tempted to think God had messed up. Encourage them to state what Psalm 147:5, found in the margin of Day 1, declares about God. Inquire: *Does a wise parent always explain his or her rationale for everything to a child? When do you have to say to a child, "Trust me; I know what I'm doing?" When has God said that to you?* Complete the last activity of Day 1. Determine how the truth that God is completely in control helps participants trust Him. Ask: *How can we deal with tragedies we just can't understand?* Allow time for discussion.

4. Request someone read aloud Colossians 2:6. Discuss the first activity of Day 2. Ask: *If we received Christ by faith, how are we to walk in Christ?* After learners answer, "By faith," then ask, *What does that mean?*

NOTES

Complete the final activity of Day 2. Ask participants if they feel like they always please God with their faith and why. Invite someone to read aloud Luke 22:31-34. Examine how Peter must have felt after he denied the Lord. Ask: *Did Jesus give up on Peter because of his failure and lack of trust?* Briefly detail Jesus' restoration of Peter in John 21. Declare: *When you walk by faith, you recognize that God never gives up on you. You can trust Him on that.*

5. Ask what it takes to live by faith. Discuss the first activity of Day 3. Speculate what doubts might have gone through Noah's and Abraham's minds. Ask: *What kept them going? What was the reward for their obedience?* Discuss the second and third activities of Day 3. Explore how believers shrink back from trusting God.

6. State that we may draw back because of barriers to our faith. Moses tried to shrink back from what God called him to do. Discuss the first activity of Day 4. Read aloud Exodus 3:12a and 14a. State that God replied that it didn't matter who Moses was. What mattered was who God is and what He would do. Explore why ignorance of who God is is a barrier to faith. Complete the second activity of Day 4. Read aloud Exodus 4:2-5 to see how God responded to Moses' doubt. Invite someone to read aloud Exodus 4:10-15. Guide the class to determine two of Moses' greatest barriers to faith and how God responded to each. State that God would not let Moses shrink back from His purposes. Determine why we don't need to shrink back according to Ephesians 3:20-21.

7. State that we can learn how to express a stepping-forward faith from the story of David and Goliath. Complete the first activity of Day 5. Read aloud 1 Samuel 17:32-37. Ask what David concluded from past victories. Determine from 1 Samuel 17:26 David's motive for fighting Goliath. Complete the third activity of Day 5 and explore why David didn't lose faith. Discuss the fourth activity of Day 5. Discuss how David responded to the challenge with positive confessions. Explore various "Goliaths" we as adults face in our lives and the positive confessions we can make about those giants.

8. Close by praying the prayer in the margin of page 51.

Obedience Always Brings Blessing

day One

The Key to God's Heart, Part 1

Some people believe the key to God's heart is love, or faith, or service. I want to tell you that *the key to God's heart is obedience.* Since obedience is what God asks of us, obedience should be a priority for anyone who desires to know God and please Him. It is always the right choice, with no exceptions. Jesus said, "If anyone loves me, he will obey my teaching. My Father will love him, and we will come to him and make our home with him" (John 14:23, NIV).

Obedience is critical to the successful Christian life, and there are several truths found in Luke 5:1–11 that will help you understand it from a divine perspective.

> **Read Luke 5:1-11 in your Bible and identify the verse that contains:**
> • a small request = verse _____
> • an "unreasonable" request = verse _____
> • a dramatic request = verse _____

1. OBEYING GOD IN SMALL MATTERS IS AN ESSENTIAL STEP TO GOD'S GREATEST BLESSINGS

Suppose Peter had said, "I'm busy cleaning my nets right now. I can't help You because I'm going fishing again tonight—I just don't have the time." Or he could have said, "Why don't You ask to use that other boat over there?" or "I've already been fishing today. It would be a waste of time to go again right now." If Peter had said anything other than yes, he would have missed the greatest fishing experience of his life. But because of Peter's obedience, the Lord arranged a miracle that he would never forget.

Oftentimes God's greatest blessings come as a result of our willingness to do something that appeared to be very insignificant. So ask yourself, *Has God been challenging me to do something seemingly unimportant that I have not yet made an effort to accomplish? Is there anything I have rationalized by saying, "It's too difficult," "I don't want to," or even "I have to pray about it"?*

2. OUR OBEDIENCE IS ALWAYS BENEFICIAL TO OTHERS

Think of all the people who were blessed by Peter's obedience. In addition to the crowd being able to see the Lord and hear His lesson, Jesus Himself benefited: preaching from the boat afforded Him the comfort of being able to sit down while He spoke (v. 3). Not only that, but Peter's friends had a very profitable day—they took in two boats so full of fish that both began to sink. More important, they had the opportunity to witness something supernatural.

God often rewards other people—especially those closest to us—as a result of our obedience. For example, no father can be obedient to God without blessing pouring out into the lives of his wife and his children. And a child's obedience will likewise bless his or her parents.

3. OBEYING GOD MAY REQUIRE DOING SOME THINGS THAT APPEAR TO BE UNREASONABLE

Peter was a skillful fisherman who knew all the best fishing spots and understood the optimal times and conditions for a catch. Then Jesus, an itinerant preacher and carpenter, approached the seasoned seaman and said, "Let's go fishing." Peter must have been thinking, *He is certainly a wonderful teacher, but I'm the fisherman. We fished all night long with no success, and besides, it is now midday, the worst possible time to net anything.* To his credit, Peter chose to obey (v. 5) and, as a result, experienced a stunning display of divine power.

Our obedience to God should never be based on whether something seems rational or fits with the world's way of thinking. That is not to say God always bypasses common sense, but oftentimes what He requires of us may not appear reasonable or match our preconceived ideas.

4. WHEN WE OBEY GOD, WE WILL NEVER BE DISAPPOINTED

Because of his experience at fishing, Peter undoubtedly assumed Jesus' instructions would amount to killing time, waiting for nothing to happen. But when he complied with that simple request, he was gripped with amazement at what the Lord brought about.

We, like Peter, must recognize that obeying God is always the wise course of action. Jesus turned an empty boat into a full one. He can also take our emptiness—whether it is related to finance, relationship, or career—and change it into something splendid and thriving.

What's empty in your life? _____

What's the key to filling it up? _____

The Key to God's Heart, Part 2

5. OUR OBEDIENCE ALLOWS GOD TO DEMONSTRATE HIS POWER IN OUR LIVES

If Peter had said no, he would have missed an awesome demonstration of divine power that made his faith skyrocket and marked the beginning of the most thrilling three years imaginable.

Read the following passages in your Bible.
What miracles did Peter witness that were even
greater than two boatloads of fish?

Mark 10:46-52 _____

John 11:43-44 _____

Matthew 14:28-29 _____

Why do you think he had the courage to leave his vessel and walk on the water toward Christ? The reason is that Peter started by saying yes to a small request. Then each time God rewarded his obedience, the apostle's faith grew to the point that he believed his Master not only controlled the fish in the water but also had absolute authority over the water!

6. OBEYING GOD ALWAYS RESULTS IN DEEPER UNDERSTANDING

Prior to this incident, Peter might have been aware that Jesus was a carpenter. He certainly knew Him as a rabbi and had heard the profound truths the Lord taught the crowds. However, obeying Christ's request set the stage for Peter to get brand-new insight—the Lord's holiness and sovereign authority over nature were clearly evident through the miraculous catch. By contrast, the fisherman likely recognized his own sinfulness. When we obey God, we, too, will discover that something happens in our hearts.

7. OBEYING GOD WILL RESULT IN DRAMATIC CHANGES IN OUR LIVES

Simon Peter had in all likelihood intended to spend the rest of his life fishing. But everything changed with one simple act of obedience. He willingly laid down his net and walked into a whole new lifestyle of following the Lord Jesus Christ.

God can revolutionize our lives. For some people this could mean a change of career, a new location, or a different relationship. Are you willing to do what God says, when and how He says to do it? Are you willing to leave all the consequences to Him?

To become wholly surrendered disciples of Christ, we must begin by obeying Him in every aspect of our lives, however small it may seem. Remember the good servant, who heard his master say, "Well done, good slave, because you have been faithful in a very little thing, you are to be in authority over ten cities" (Luke 19:17). Unless you say yes to a little request from the Lord, you will never know what your life could have been like—or what wonderful blessing would have been yours if only you had obeyed God.

What little request has God been making of you?

_____

How will you respond today? _____

The Priority of Obedience

We must place obedience to God at the top of our priority list. But to do so, we need to fully understand why obedience plays such an important role in our relationship with God. To illustrate this, I want to discuss people in the Bible who approached obedience in very different ways.

DISOBEDIENCE: ADAM AND EVE

Disobedience always brings about painful consequences. Sometimes those consequences affect only the individual who sins, and sometimes they affect others. Perhaps the clearest illustration of this truth comes from the story of Adam and Eve.

God created a perfect environment for this young couple and gave them just two commands: "Be fruitful and multiply" (Gen. 1:28), and "From the tree of the knowledge of good and evil you shall not eat" (Gen. 2:17). We know that Adam and his wife understood these simple instructions because Eve was able to repeat them to the tempter prior to succumbing to his evil plan (Gen. 3:3).

Disobedience is rebellion against God—irreverence toward Him. It is a statement from your heart proclaiming that you have chosen your way over God's way. When you are disobedient, you are essentially refusing to acknowledge God's authority, right, and power in your life. To avoid disobedience, when God gives you words of direction, wisdom, or warning, you must heed them completely.

PARTIAL OBEDIENCE: KING SAUL

Obeying God requires *exact* and *total* obedience. When we turn to 1 Samuel 10, we can follow the case of King Saul and his struggle with total obedience.

Saul received God's instructions to go to Gilgal and wait seven days for the prophet Samuel to join him. The two would then make a burnt offering together (1 Sam. 10:8). Saul started well, but as the seventh day approached, he became restless and frustrated, and finally decided to make an offering without Samuel.

Read 1 Samuel 13:5-14 in your Bible.
What happened as soon as Saul made the offering?

_____

What was Saul's rationale for his actions? _____

What was the result? _____

Saul waited *almost* long enough, but partial obedience is not obedience.

God does not promise that we will be able to see or understand how His plan for our lives is to unfold. Instead, He often calls us to obey Him moment by moment, trusting Him to pull all the pieces together in His timing. Many times we will have to wait, but when we do so in obedience, God will bless the outcome.

COMPLETE OBEDIENCE: NOAH

When we read about the life of Noah in Genesis 6–9, we see a clear picture of *complete* obedience. When God called this man to do something extraordinary—a task that seemed both impossible and illogical—Noah complied without asking questions. Noah obeyed God despite what other people thought of him. And when we choose the path of obedience, we must likewise be prepared for the negative responses we will undoubtedly receive from others.

Will it always be popular for you to obey God? No, it will not. Will people criticize you? Yes, they probably will. Might they think some things that you do are ridiculous? Yes. Will they sometimes laugh at you? Yes. Noah chose to walk with God in the midst of a corrupt society. In fact, it was so wicked that God chose to destroy every living human being on the face of the earth with the exception of one family.

From the life of Noah, we can deduce an important key to obedience: When God tells us to do something, we must not focus on the circumstances or the persons who would deter us from carrying out God's instructions. If Noah had begun to listen to his critics, he would not have built the ark, and he would have been swept away with the rest of the earth. Instead, he chose to be absolutely obedient to God.

My prayer for you is that you will be obedient to God. That way you can become the person He wants you to be, do the work He desires of you, bear the fruit He enables you to bear, and receive the blessings He has prepared for you.

Circle the category that best defines your obedience.
Disobedience   **Partial**   **Complete**

How might your obedience be affecting the degree to which you are living the extraordinary life?

_____

day *Four*

The Joy of Obedience

"In truth, nothing good can come from disobeying God, and nothing bad can come from obeying Him."—Charles Stanley

In commanding us to obey Him, God has given us a principle by which to live. He has set a framework for our lives that forms a hedge of protection from evil. God's concern for us springs from His deep love and devotion. He commands our obedience not because He is a strict taskmaster but because He knows the effect that disobedience and sin will have on our lives. In truth, nothing good can come from disobeying God, and nothing bad can come from obeying Him.

Read Isaiah 48:17-19 in the margin. Then list good things that come from obeying God.

Satan has a different goal in mind. He knows that if he can entice us to sin, our actions will dishonor the Lord and bring sorrow to the heart of God. Disobedience also has fierce repercussions. Feelings of guilt, shame, and worthlessness are just a few of the emotional consequences. Broken lives, destroyed marriages, and bitter disputes also happen when we disobey.

Sin alienates believers from God's blessings. In times of disobedience, we become spiritually weak and unable to discern right from wrong. Many times we are unable to reverse our sinful behavior and thereby sink deeper into its grasp.

God does not leave us hopeless, however. God has provided all we need to say no to temptation (1 Cor. 10:13). Despite the fact that Satan's enticements lead to fretting, lying, or negative thoughts, God's Word is an infinite resource of truth, hope, and assurance. We do not have to yield to sin because God is always in control. He stays close to us and is personally involved in all we do. He understands our deepest needs and heartfelt longings.

The Book of Deuteronomy chronicles Israel's preparation to enter the promised land.

"Thus says the LORD, your Redeemer, the Holy One of Israel, 'I am the LORD your God, who teaches you to profit, who leads you in the way you should go. If only you had paid attention to My commandments! Then your well-being would have been like a river, and your righteousness like the waves of the sea. Your descendants would have been like the sand, and your offspring like its grains; Their name would never be cut off or destroyed from My presence' " (Isa. 48:17-19, NASB).

Read Deuteronomy 11:26-28 in your Bible.

God's people would be blessed if they _____

and cursed if they _____.

Chapter 28 spells out the blessings that would come as a result of Israel's obedience. This same principle is at work in our lives. Obedience leads to God's blessing while disobedience leads to disappointment, sorrow, and brokenness.

How to Get Started

You begin a life of obedience when you apply the following principles to your life.

TRUST GOD WITH YOUR LIFE AND LEAVE THE CONSEQUENCES TO HIM

There is no way to go wrong if you place your hope and trust in God. He created you, and He loves you with an eternal love. You are His greatest concern, and He will never give you second best (Prov. 3:5–6).

LEARN TO WAIT ON THE LORD

When in doubt, refuse to move ahead unless you know that God is leading you. When you jump ahead of God and make the decision to act without clear instruction from Him, you are disobeying Him (Ps. 27:14; 62:1–8).

"My soul waits in silence for God only; From Him is my salvation....
My soul, wait in silence for God only, for my hope is from Him"
(Ps. 62:1,5, NASB).

Read Psalm 62:1,5 in the margin. Circle how we are to wait on God. Underline why we are to wait.

LEARN TO MEDITATE ON GOD'S WORD

Prayer and meditation are key elements in resisting temptation. When you saturate your mind with the Word of God, you will gain God's viewpoint concerning your life and situation. Therefore, when temptation comes, you will know right from wrong and can act accordingly.

LEARN TO LISTEN TO THE HOLY SPIRIT

Many wonder if God speaks to His people today. The answer is yes. He speaks to us through His Word, by His Spirit, and in the counsel of a pastor or a trusted Christian friend. Actually the Spirit of God is the One who draws us to Scripture and points out passages that God seeks to use in our lives. Seek Him through His Word, and spend time with Him by praying and studying the principles written in Scripture.

BE WILLING TO WALK AWAY WHEN THE PATH IS UNCERTAIN

Obedience to God will require you to be firm if you desire to please Him above all others. If you do not sense clear guidance for your situation, ask God to confirm His will to you in His Word. He will never go against Scripture. His intentions for your life always will line up perfectly with what is written in the Bible.

BE WILLING TO EXPERIENCE CONFLICT

God rarely empties our lives of trouble and conflict. If He did, our dependence on Him would fade. He allows enough difficulty to keep us turned toward Him (John 16:33). Many times your obedience will not be viewed as popular, especially if you take a certain stand against the peer pressure of the world. But it will put you in a favorable position before God, and just as He promised to bless the nation of Israel, He will do the same for you.

ACCEPT GOD'S DISCIPLINE WITH THANKSGIVING

In the story of the prodigal son (Luke 15:11–32) we read of God's love and forgiveness toward us. While the consequences of sin are unavoidable, we can experience true forgiveness and renewed hope when we turn back to God. Perhaps you have made a wrong decision. God may not remove all the heartache and pain your decision has caused, but He can forgive you and restore His blessing in your life. When we turn to Him in repentance, He will wash sin's darkness from our lives (Ps. 51:7).

Dr. Stanley wrote, "Making a commitment to obey God is essential to our faith."

Do you commit today to obey God in all things?
❑ **Yes**   ❑ **No**   ❑ **I'm getting there**

Sign your name to solidify your commitment.

**Prayer:
Dear Father in heaven, I ask Your forgiveness for my self-sufficiency and for all the times I hear Your commands yet fail to obey them. I purpose to align my life with Your principles and to obey Your Word. Please help me in this pursuit and convict me when I stray. Amen.**

leader Guide

To the Leader:

List ways God has blessed you for your obedience.

Spend time thanking Him for calling you and blessing you with this awesome responsibility of teaching learners the faith.

Make it a point to affirm class participants for their obedience to attend and participate in Bible study.

During the Session

1. Ask what we mean when we say something is the key to someone's heart. Ask: *What's the key to your heart?* OR Ask participants how many keys they have in their purse/pocket. Request they turn to the person next to them and identify what each key opens. FOR EITHER OPTION: Ask learners to identify what Dr. Stanley said is the key to God's heart. Request someone read aloud John 14:23. State that obedience is also the key to open our hearts so Jesus can come in and make His home there. Ask what obedience brings and why that would be a principle for living the extraordinary life.

2. Complete the first activity of Day 1. Request someone read aloud the first truth about obeying God. Invite volunteers to share times they have experienced God's greatest blessings because of their willingness to do something seemingly insignificant. Discuss who benefited from Peter's obedience. Ask how Peter might have wanted to respond to Jesus' instructions to put out his nets again. Inquire: *How did Peter discover truth #4?* Discuss what is empty in people's lives today. Ask: *What's the key to filling up that emptiness?* Allow time for discussion.

3. Surmise what Peter would have missed if he had chosen the reasonable route and ignored the Lord's instructions. Invite volunteers to share how they have observed God's power when they were obedient to Him. Determine what deeper understanding Peter gained because of his obedience. Ask: *How has obedience given you a deeper understanding of God and yourself? How does that lead to extraordinary living?* Ask why, with all these benefits of obeying, we still hesitate to obey God.

4. State that despite our hesitation we must place obedience to God at the top of our priority list because it's the key to blessing. Ask what two commands God gave Adam and Eve. Ask: *Were those huge, unreasonable requests? Why then did they disobey?* Request someone read aloud Romans 5:12-14. Determine the consequence of Adam and Eve's sin and who was affected. Read aloud 1 Samuel 10:1-8. Complete the first activity of Day 3. Evaluate how believers try to get away with partial disobedience. Ask why partial obedience really isn't obedience at all.

Lead the group to determine how Noah is an illustration of complete obedience. State that there is another category of obedience and that is ultimate obedience. Read aloud Philippians 2:5-8. Request someone read aloud Romans 5:18-19. Lead the class to determine who was affected by Jesus' obedience. Acknowledge that some might think that following Jesus' example won't lead to extraordinary living since His obedience led to death. But there's more to the story. Read aloud Philippians 2:9-11. Urge participants to use the final activity of Day 3 to evaluate their obedience. Then discuss the final question as a group.

5. Complete the last activity of Day 4. Assess the curses, damages, and consequences that Moses stated would result from disobedience. Then discuss the first activity of Day 4. To further examine blessings God promised as a result of obedience, organize the class into two groups. Direct the first group to list from Deuteronomy 28:1-6 promised blessings of obedience. Instruct the second group to do the same with Deuteronomy 28:7-14. (OPTION: You may want to have participants list the curses resulting from disobedience that are found in the remainder of Deuteronomy 28.) Ask: *What is the joy of obedience?* Allow time for discussion.

6. Ask: *What kind of relationship must we have with our children if they are going to obey us with the right attitude? Why is trusting God with our lives and leaving the consequences to Him an essential first step in obedience?* Complete the first activity in Day 5. Explore what it means to wait in silence. Remark that part of waiting silently is meditating on God's Word. Allow volunteers to share how prayer and focusing on God's Word have empowered them to obey when it was very difficult to do so. Read aloud John 10:27. Declare that if we are going to follow Jesus in obedience then we must learn to listen to His voice. Help learners determine how God speaks to believers today and how we can know it's Him. Ask: *Why must we be willing to experience conflict if we commit to obedience? What can encourage us even during that conflict? What's our hope if we have been disobedient to God?*

7. Urge learners to prayerfully consider and then complete the closing activity on page 63.

8. Then ask learners to silently pray the closing prayer found in the margin of page 63.

Knowing God's Will Is Worth the Wait

day One

Learning the Art of Active Waiting

Waiting is essential in living the Christian life. God always has a very clear reason for telling us to wait, and the reason is without exception to our benefit.

Being patient is surely difficult, but failing to wait upon the Lord can bring about disastrous consequences. First, when we do not wait, we get out of God's will. Second, we delay God's planned blessing for us. Because we move ahead of His steps, we get out of cycle and miss God's blessings in His time. Third, we bring pain and suffering upon others and ourselves. Throughout Scripture you can see the resulting pain that people endure from getting out of God's will and doing things their own way. Fourth, we are prone to make snap judgments that quite often turn out to cost us dearly in terms of finances, emotional energy, and/or relationships.

Waiting on the Lord, however, does not mean being stagnant. Thus it is important for you to realize what it means to truly wait upon the Lord.

First, waiting upon the Lord does not require you to be idle. Instead, it simply means pausing until you receive further instructions. You should think of waiting as a determined stillness, during which time you decide not to act until the Lord gives clear direction.

Second, in Scripture God often instructs His people to wait.

As you read Psalm 27:14 and 37:4-7, printed in the margin, underline what is essential in waiting on God.

Sometimes it takes a great deal of courage to wait and wait as you start to think, *If I don't take advantage of this opportunity now, I'm going to*

"Wait for the LORD; Be strong and let your heart take courage; Yes, wait for the LORD" (Ps. 27:14, NASB).

"Delight yourself in the LORD; and He will give you the desires of your heart. Commit your way to the LORD, trust also in Him, and He will do it. He will bring forth your righteousness as the light and your judgment as the noonday. Rest in the LORD and wait patiently for Him" (Ps. 37:4–7, NASB).

miss it. Yet God says, "Let your heart take courage; yes, wait for the Lord." The only way to wait patiently is to rest in Him; you must trust Him to the point that you are no longer anxious. Clearly, then, you cannot separate waiting upon the Lord and trusting in Him; these two things go hand in hand.

Third, your waiting should be marked by silence: "My soul, wait in silence for God only, for my hope is from Him. He only is my rock and my salvation, my stronghold; I shall not be shaken. (Ps. 62:5–6).

How often do you find yourself waiting and yet not being very silent about it? Oftentimes you may wait but complain about it; other times you may wait but tell God why you think He ought to hurry up. Would you agree that most of the time God is a little too slow for your schedule? You must trust enough to wait in silence.

Fourth, God will strengthen you through your waiting. See the promise in Isaiah 40:31: "Yet those who wait for the LORD will gain new strength; They will mount up with wings like eagles, they will run and not get tired, they will walk and not become weary."

Does that mean that you will never get weary? No, of course not. It's one thing to be tired *in* your labors; it's something else to be tired *of* your labors, which is to become weary on the inside. You can go a long way even though you may be weary on the outside. However, when you have no one in whom to trust, your spirit becomes weary, and that is a far worse predicament.

Fifth, waiting does not involve looking around to see what others are doing. How often have you been sure of what the Lord has said to do, but then changed your course of action because of what you saw others doing around you? Or how often have you been sure of what the Lord has said, but then begun to doubt Him because of the negative voices you heard?

When it comes to your personal, private walk with God, this is the bottom line: Are you going to listen to God and do what He says? Are you going to wait upon Him when your peers become impatient and everything around you is pushing you to move?

Waiting demands patience, and it certainly requires trust. As you wait upon the Lord, you will have to stand strong against the pressure of other people who want to goad you into making a decision that fits their schedules and timing. If God has not given you the green light, moving forward at the insistence of others is the worst thing you can do.

Read Micah 7:1-8 in your Bible. What was Micah's . . .

Dilemma? _____

Determination?_____

Destiny? _____

Yes, waiting is hard. It is difficult to stand still when everything in you wants to move. However, wise men and women wait upon the Lord until they have heard from Him. Then, when they finally move, it is with boldness, confidence, courage, strength, and absolute assurance that God will keep His word.

day *Two*

When God Doesn't Seem to Answer

There are times in every Christian's life when God seems distant and uninterested in the circumstances. We pray and diligently seek His will, but our need, at least from our perspective, remains unmet. How should we handle times of spiritual silence when we feel as though God is standing at a distance and is not going to answer our prayers?

Consider the story of Mary, Martha, and Lazarus in John 11. The issue in the story is not one of healing—it is one of need and how God met the need.

Read in your Bible John 11:1-16.

What was the need? _____

How did Jesus initially respond?_____

How might Martha and Mary have interpreted Jesus'

delay? _____

Sometimes when we have to wait for God's provision or answer, it seems as if He is completely uninterested in our situation. Many times we lose patience with God and attempt to meet our own unmet needs. In so doing, we often make matters worse by resorting to the following:

DENIAL

We tell ourselves there is not a problem. While denial is an initial defense we use to protect ourselves from the reality of deep tragedy, a prolonged period of denial is not healthy. We need to face reality with God, knowing that He has a solution for the problems we encounter.

AVOIDANCE

We distance ourselves from the problem in an attempt to protect ourselves from further pain. Avoidance works for a short time. We can see how God used it in the lives of His saints to provide brief intervals of rest. However, just like denial, avoidance prevents us from dealing with the problem. The solution is to seek God for wisdom and a precise way to handle our circumstances, even if this includes waiting for Him to lead us beyond this moment in time. Be willing to wait for God's best. Jumping ahead of Him leads only to more confusion.

PROJECTION

We use projection when we blame others. God is completely aware of your situation. He knows exactly what you are facing, and He knows how you will react. This is why it is crucial for you to turn to Him for wisdom and for the right response.

Read John 11:17-37 in your Bible. Do you think Martha and Mary (check one)
❏ **Blamed Jesus?**
❏ **Stated a fact?**
❏ **Expressed their trust in His power?**

LYING

When we avoid telling the truth, we end up hurting others and ourselves. There is only one way to handle the trials of life and that is truthfully. We do not have to disclose all we know or feel, however.

God wants us to be careful with our words. Lying and rationalization do not help solve the problem. They only hinder a final, godly resolution.

GIVING IN AND GIVING UP

When trials come, we are faced with the temptation to quit. Discouragement is one of Satan's favorite forms of attack. He believes that if he can discourage us, we will give up and turn away from God's will and plan for our lives. Never give up! Trust God to the end, and you will see His goodness become a reality in your life.

Read John 11:38-44 in your Bible. What emotions do you think Martha and Mary experienced . . .

During their four-day wait for Jesus? _____

After the wait? _____

CONFORMITY

Rather than stand for what we know is right, we can easily conform to the situation under pressure. Our initiative and creativity drain away, and we run the risk of sinking into depression.

day Three

How Should You Handle Your Unmet Needs?

BEGIN WITH PRAYER.

Let your needs be made known to God (Phil. 4:6). Jesus taught His disciples that prayer is a lifestyle, not just an activity in which you participate. When you feel overwhelmed by your circumstances, prayer is the one way to change the direction of your mind and heart. It places your focus on God, who is the only Source of hope and truth.

ACKNOWLEDGE YOUR NEED & THE BURDEN YOU ARE CARRYING

The saints of the church used an endearing phrase when they talked about giving their problems to God in prayer. They said, "Roll your burden over onto the Lord." This is your hope.

Read Lamentations 3:18-26 in your Bible.

Why had the writer lost hope? _____

What renewed his hope?_____

CLAIM GOD'S PROMISES

When you are facing a difficult situation, train yourself to appropriate divine promises. Scripture is your greatest source of encouragement. Claiming God's promises and remaining committed to the course He has given you is a powerful way to face any tribulation or change.

SEEK GOD'S DIRECTION

You can seek God's direction through the study of His Word and through prayer. Ask Him to help you distinguish between the real need and what you perceive as a need. Make sure that your motives are pure and God-centered rather than self-centered. Ask Him to tear down any barriers that separate you from Him.

BE WILLING TO WAIT

This is crucial. What was the greater miracle: healing Lazarus or bringing him back to life after he was dead for four days? God always has a greater good in mind.

Read John 11:4,40-42 in your Bible. What was the greater good God had in mind with Lazarus's death?

_____

THANK GOD IN ADVANCE FOR HIS PROVISION

Thanking God for His faithfulness and provision is an indication of your submission to His will regardless of your hopes or expectations.

If you desire to dig deeper...

Read the following promises from God's Words.

Circle those that are especially meaningful at this point in your life.

Psalm 30:5

Proverbs 3:5-10; 16:3

Isaiah 41:10; 43:2; 48:17

Matthew 11:28

Romans 8:1

2 Corinthians 4:8-9

Galatians 6:9

Philippians 4:6-7,13,19

James 4:7

1 John 4:4; 5:4-5

71

Why Is It Wise to Wait?

1. TO RECEIVE GOD'S CLEAR DIRECTION FOR YOUR LIFE

Can you name anything you should not share with God? Everything deserves His attention. The Lord desires you to sift everything through His will, purpose, plan, and Word.

2. TO KEEP IN STEP WITH GOD'S TIMING

Your timing may not be the same as God's. So, even though God intends for you to have a blessing, He may withhold it for a time and say, "No, this is not the right time to proceed."

3. TO ALLOW GOD THE PROPER TIME TO PREPARE YOU FOR HIS ANSWER

"I am weary with my crying; my throat is parched; My eyes fail while I wait for my God… But as for me, my prayer is to You, O LORD, at an acceptable time; O God, in the greatness of Your lovingkindness, answer me with Your saving truth" (Ps. 69:3,13, NASB).

Sometimes God has to prepare you for the blessing or the next move. What would be a delight for you tomorrow might be an absolute disaster today.

Read Psalm 69:3,13, printed in the margin. Write the phrase below that demonstrates the psalmist was willing to wait on God's timing.

_____

4. TO STRENGTHEN YOUR FAITH IN HIM

Think about how Abraham felt. God had promised a son, but decades passed without a child. Had Abraham heard God incorrectly? No, because we know that Abraham became the father of the entire Hebrew nation. Abraham was not perfect, but through years of waiting he learned to trust the Lord.

5. To Allow God to Sift Through Your Motives to Reveal Your Desires

Even if what you want meshes with what God wants, your motives may be poorly aligned. What is your motive? Is it something selfish? God often makes His people wait so He may take time to clean their hearts of poor motives.

Read Psalm 40:1-3 in your Bible. How did the psalmist discover it was wise to wait on God?

_____

Benefits of Following God's Will

The benefits of following God's will—and the consequences of ignoring it—are compelling reasons to search out what the Lord desires for your life. When making important decisions, consider the following questions:

1. Is It Consistent with the Word of God?

Look for Scripture that either indicates this is the right way to go or gives you reason not to proceed. Even if you cannot find verses describing a situation comparable to yours, look for applicable truths. God's Word is full of life principles; a single passage can offer wisdom that applies to many circumstances.

2. Is This A Wise Decision?

To answer this question, you must ask yourself several others: *What are the future consequences? Am I rushing into something? Where is this going to take me? Will it create debt? Will it harm anyone?* As you begin to ask these questions, the Holy Spirit will bear witness to your spirit whether moving ahead is right or wrong.

3. CAN I HONESTLY ASK GOD TO ENABLE ME TO ACHIEVE THIS?

Some people will tell you it is OK to ask God for anything, but that is not the case. Even if you need money badly, you cannot ask God to permit a deceptive or fraudulent scheme. Remember, anything you acquire outside of God's will sooner or later turns to ashes.

4. DO I HAVE A GENUINE PEACE ABOUT THIS?

Colossians 3:15 declares, "Let the peace of Christ rule in your hearts." But what does it mean to have peace? You cannot force peace, but you can know when it is genuine. And remember, God simply will not give us any peace about something that is not His will.

5. DOES THIS FIT WHO I AM AS A FOLLOWER OF JESUS?

Some things just do not fit a child of God. If we claim to be Christians, it would not be fitting to hold a grudge, gossip, have inappropriate relationships, or express unduly harsh criticism.

6. DOES THIS FIT GOD'S OVERALL PLAN FOR MY LIFE?

We need to consider how our thinking, conduct, and here-and-now decisions coincide with the Lord's long-range plans for us. This is why we must teach our children to be very careful about how they decide upon a vocation, choose a marriage partner, and make all the other major decisions of life. In each instance, the question is, *Does this fit God's purpose for my life?*

7. WILL THIS DECISION HONOR GOD?

Am I showing respect and reverence for the Heavenly Father by taking this course of action? Is it evident by what I am doing that I acknowledge Jesus Christ as the Lord and Master of my life? Our actions and attitudes should be in keeping with who we know God to be rather than a statement that we are "doing our own thing." Our disobedience grieves the heart of God, but He is not the only One who notices. The world watches Christians to see if we are consistent or hypocritical, so it is important that our decisions reflect an obedient heart toward the Lord.

What important decision or struggle are you dealing with right now? _____

Prayerfully apply the previous seven questions to that decision.

Considered honestly, these seven questions reveal a lot about what is in your heart, and they also help you to discover the heart of God. Once you know God's mind on a matter, there is one final question to ask yourself: *Now that I know His will, am I willing to do it?*

If you are in the process of making a difficult decision and are frightened about the consequences, remember that you have entrusted your life to a loving Heavenly Father who plans only the best, promises only the best, and provides only the best. You simply cannot lose when you obey the will of God.

Read Isaiah 25:6-9, printed in the margin. What is the ultimate benefit of waiting on God?

_____

_____

Prayer:

Lord, I pray that You will teach me how to wait on You for Your perfect timing. I turn over to You all of my expectations and trust that You will bring about what is best for me at the right time. Amen.

"The LORD of hosts will prepare a lavish banquet for all peoples on this mountain… He will swallow up death for all time, and the Lord GOD will wipe tears away from all faces, and He will remove the reproach of His people from all the earth; for the LORD has spoken. And it will be said in that day, 'Behold, this is our God for whom we have waited that He might save us. This is the LORD for whom we have waited; Let us rejoice and be glad in His salvation' " (Isa. 25:6,8-9, NASB).

To the Leader:

Look at your meeting space through the eyes of a visitor. Do you need to remove some clutter? hang some posters to add a little color to the walls? Can chairs be rearranged to encourage more eye-to-eye discussion?

Before the Session

Make or purchase a coffee cake. Prepare a tray of fruit.

During the Session

1. Ask participants to name some things in life that are worth the wait. OR Offer coffee cake and fruit to participants. As participants enjoy their refreshments, ask what role waiting played in the cake and fruit they are eating. Ask: *Would the cake be any good if the baker grew impatient and removed it from the oven before it was time? Would the fruit be any good if the farmer impatiently picked it before it was ripe? Would you agree that waiting is an essential part of life? Why?* FOR EITHER OPTION Ask: *If we acknowledge that some things in life are definitely worth the wait, why do most of us hate waiting for anything?* Announce that the sixth principle for living the extraordinary life recognizes that knowing God's will is worth the wait.

2. Ask: *Will we always know the reasons God has us wait? What can we know about the God-ordained waits in our lives?* [They are always for our benefit.] Guide the class to state consequences of failing to wait on God to find a spouse, determine a career path, make a large purchase [add your own items here]. Review the consequences Dr. Stanley listed in Day 1 for failing to wait on God. Declare that since failing to wait on God is so disastrous, His children must learn the art of active waiting. Lead the class to determine the difference between waiting in determined stillness and sitting around doing nothing. Discuss the first activity of Day 1. Review the remaining three essentials to active waiting discussed in Day 1. Complete the final activity of Day 1. Ask: *Why did Micah need courage to wait on God? How are our situations similar to Micah's? What must be our determination?*

3. Acknowledge that we find it hard to wait when God doesn't seem to hear or care about us. Use the three activities in Day 2 to study a biblical account of having to wait on God to act. Urge participants not to make matters worse in difficult times by resorting to the defense mechanisms discussed in Day 2.

4. State: *Somewhere along the line, Martha and Mary had to accept God's will over their own. We're each going to face that decision. So, how can we handle our unmet needs so God's perfect will is accomplished in our lives?* To answer that question, organize the class into three groups. Instruct Group 1 to use Philippians 4:6-7 and the first activity of Day 3 to explore the first two ways of dealing with unmet needs discussed in Day 3. Instruct Group 2 to do the same with the third way, using the activity in the margin. Have Group 3 discuss the final three ways using James 4:1-3 and the final activity of Day 3. Allow groups time to share and discuss what they discovered.

5. Request groups stay together. Ask volunteers to state from Day 4 reasons why it is wise to wait. Instruct all three groups to read Psalm 37. Instruct Group 1 to list from the psalm characteristics of a waiting believer. Ask Group 2 to list God's promises to a waiting believer. Have Group 3 identify the end results for a waiting believer. Request groups share their lists. Allow time for discussion.

6. Invite volunteers to read aloud the seven questions believers must ask themselves when making important decisions. Ask if participants would add any questions to that list. Consider how asking those questions may mean a believer may have to wait on God.

7. Read aloud Luke 14:27-33. Evaluate with learners the costs of waiting to discern God's will and then doing His will once you know it. Ask: *Is knowing God's will worth the wait? Why or why not?*

8. Discuss the final activity of Day 5.

9. Pray the prayer at the conclusion of Day 5 as your closing prayer.

After the Session

Meet with class leaders to evaluate how your class is meeting needs through outreach to prospects and visitors, in-reach to class participants in their times of need, and fellowship through class activities. Plan a fellowship activity that will take place before Thanksgiving. Go ahead and put your class Christmas party on the calendar. It's not too early to begin considering a mission project your class wants to participate in for the holiday season.

God Refines Us By Fire

day One

God Is in Control

Cloth can dust off a piece of gold, but the metal must be refined to remove embedded impurities. That is, it must be melted by fire so that any tarnish or pollution can rise and be skimmed from the surface.

The Christian life is frequently compared to this process.

Read the following passages in your Bible and note what God does with His people and why.

Zechariah 13:9 _____

_____

Malachi 3:2-4 _____

_____

When we face struggles, God is refining us like precious metal, digging deep into our lives to eliminate all the dirt and pollution. He does this not to hurt us but to help us grow into beautiful reflections of Him.

I remember a particular time when I was struggling with discouragement, doubt, fear, and loneliness. I spent many evenings having long conversations with a close friend to whom I poured out my heart for hours. Many times during these talks, my friend stopped me and said, "But remember, God is in control." This statement became an anchor in my life. No matter how hard the winds blew or how much the adversity intensified, my soul remained anchored to the simple truth: God is in control. I discovered that when a person is able to face terrifying obstacles with the assurance of God's complete control, an awesome sense of power and assurance begins to well up inside his heart.

The psalmist David learned this lesson through ups and downs, successes and fierce challenges. David praised God for His sovereignty, crying out, "The LORD has established His throne in the heavens; and His sovereignty rules over all" (Ps. 103:19).

Read each of the passages listed below in your Bible. Draw a line to match the reference with the entities over which God rules (it may be more than one).

Sovereignty is . . . "God's supreme and absolute rule, control and authority over this entire universe and every single human being."— Charles Stanley, *Living the Extraordinary Life,* page 131.

Job 12:23-25	**The world's water supply**
Psalm 22:28	**Heaven and earth**
Psalm 104:10-14	**The world's food supply**
Psalm 135:6-7	**The world's nations and leaders**

Because we know God is in control, we can find peace in several assurances from the Father. First, we find comfort in the fact that almighty God is intimately and continually involved in our individual lives every single day. God never stops providing for, protecting, watching over, or caring for each of us.

Because God is sovereign, we have the assurance that He will work out every single circumstance in our lives for something good, no matter what. It may be painful, difficult, or seemingly impossible, but God can and will use that situation to achieve His divine purpose. Romans 8:28 makes this clear: "We know that God causes all things to work together for good to those who love God, to those who are called according to His purpose." This claim makes sense only when we realize that God is in complete control.

We have the assurance that nothing can touch us apart from the permissive will of God. Psalm 34:7 explains, "The angel of the LORD encamps around those who fear Him, and rescues them." God is our Protector. When something happens that is painful or unexplainable in our lives, does that mean God lost control for a moment? No, because we know that these things cannot happen unless God allows them. This hope enables us to step boldly into the future because we know that God will be there for us, forever protecting us and guiding our steps.

My friend, no matter what pain, trial, or tragedy comes your way, rejoice that your Father will be there to work it out for your good, no matter what.

Growing Stronger Through Trials

Adversity is one of life's inescapable experiences, and not one of us is ever happy when it affects us personally. A popular theology says, "Just trust God and think rightly; then you won't have hardship." In searching the Scriptures, however, we see that God has advanced His greatest servants through adversity, not prosperity.

Read Romans 5:3-4 in your Bible. Then trace the progression backward, beginning with hope in verse 4.

Hope is produced by _____, which is

produced by _____, which is produced by

_____.

God isn't interested in building a generation of fainthearted Christians. Instead, He uses trials to train up stalwart, spirit-filled soldiers for Jesus Christ. Most of us don't even want to hear about difficulties, let alone live them, but it is far better to learn about adversity *before* you experience it than to face a hardship and wonder, *Lord, what on earth are You doing?*

We live in a fallen world so, like it or not, sin and its consequences surround us. Hardship is a part of life; it can cause discouragement and even despair, sometimes to the point of disillusionment with Christianity.

When we encounter such difficulty, we typically consider the ordeal unfair, unbelievable, and unbearable. Our attitude is usually "It's not fair, God." But we should be asking, "God, what is Your point of view?"

What is God's point of view according to James 1:2-4?

_____

If our lives were free from persecution or trials—if we had everything we wanted and no problems—what would we know about our Heavenly Father? Our view of Him would be unscriptural and most likely out of balance. Without adversity, we would never understand who God is or what He is like. How can God prove His faithfulness unless He allows some situations from which He must rescue us?

Do you want the kind of faith that is based *only* on what you have heard or read? It is never *your* truth until God works it into your life. Most of us memorized these words before we even understood their meaning: "Yea, though I walk through the valley of the shadow of death, I will fear no evil: for thou art with me" (Ps. 23:4, KJV). But the twenty-third Psalm didn't become a living reality until we found ourselves in the valley.

Adversity can be a deadly discouragement or God's greatest tool for advancing spiritual growth. Your response can make all the difference. Remember that God has a purpose for the hardship He's allowed, and it fits with His wonderful plan for your life.

Read Job 23:8-12 in your Bible. In the midst of Job's adversity, what was his . . .

Certain hope? _____

Determination? _____

If you desire to dig deeper...

Read Psalm 66 in your Bible.

List what the psalmist knew about God.

How did he gain this intimate knowledge of God? _____

"Without adversity, we would never understand who God is or what He is like."
—Charles Stanley

"Adversity can be a deadly discouragement or God's greatest tool for advancing spiritual growth. Your response can make all the difference."
—Charles Stanley

"God views adversity as a way not to hinder the saints, but to advance their spiritual growth."
—Charles Stanley

81

Advancing Through Adversity

When it comes to adversity, no one is immune. All of us have experienced the heartache, pressure, and anguish caused by hardships. Whatever form our trials may take—whether sickness, financial problems, animosity, rejection, bitterness, or anger—we tend to consider them setbacks. God, however, has a different perspective. God views adversity as a way not to hinder the saints, but to advance their spiritual growth.

When facing tribulation, we often wonder where it came from: *Is this my own doing? Is this from Satan? Or is this from You, Lord?* Regardless of the specific source, ultimately all adversity that touches a believer's life must first be sifted through the permissive will of God. That is not to say everything coming your way is the Lord's will. But God *allows* everything that occurs because He sees how even adversity will fit into His wonderful purpose for your life.

Read Isaiah 55:8-9 in your Bible. In the margin, depict or describe the truth of this verse.

God's thoughts are higher than ours, so we cannot expect to understand all that He is doing. He often takes the most painful experiences of adversity and uses them to prepare us for what lies ahead. God wants us to regard our struggles the way He does so we won't be disillusioned. Therefore, far more important than determining the source of our adversity is learning how to respond properly.

Consider Joseph, one of the very few people in the Bible about whom nothing negative is written, but whose early life is characterized by adversity. Scripture says that God was prospering Joseph in the midst of his affliction—even in a foreign jail! Every trial was part of God's equipping Joseph to become the savior of Egypt and also the savior of his own family, who would later journey there to avoid starvation.

Read in your Bible Genesis 50:15-20. Explain from the two viewpoints below why Joseph endured much adversity.

From man's point of view: _____

_____

From God's point of view: _____

_____

The Bible reveals a number of reasons the Lord allows difficulties in our lives. As we begin to comprehend His purposes, we can learn to react in ways that will strengthen rather than discourage us.

Some Reasons God Allows Adversity in Our Lives, Part 1

TO GET OUR ATTENTION

God knows when we are frozen in anger and bitterness or set on doing something our own way. He may allow adversity to sweep us off our feet. When we stand before God, stripped of our pride and self-reliance, He has our complete attention.

Saul of Tarsus, later known as the apostle Paul, had to learn a lesson this way. Proud and egotistical, he was doing everything he could to rid this earth of Christians.

Read Acts 9:1-9 in your Bible. How did God use adversity to get Saul's (Paul's) attention?

_____

Lying on the Damascus road, Saul asked, "Who are You, Lord?" (Acts 9:5). God had totally captured his attention. At the time, it must have seemed like a screeching halt to his life's work; in actuality, it was the beginning of an extraordinary preaching career.

TO REMIND US OF HIS GREAT LOVE FOR US

Let me ask you: If you moved out of God's will into sin, and He just let you have your way, would that be an expression of love? Of course not. He loves us too much to let us get by with disobedience.

The Bible realistically agrees that "no discipline is enjoyable while it is happening—it is painful!" (Heb. 12:11, NLT). Just as we lovingly discipline our children to protect them from developing harmful patterns in thinking and behavior, so our Heavenly Father trains us by discipline in order to bring about "a quiet harvest of right living" (Heb. 12:11, NLT).

The writer of Hebrews said, "My child, don't ignore it when the Lord disciplines you, and don't be discouraged when he corrects you. For the Lord disciplines those he loves, and he punishes those he accepts as his children" (12:5–6, NLT). So if you are experiencing adversity, allow it to be a reminder of God's great love for you.

FOR SELF-EXAMINATION

When God allowed Satan to buffet Paul with a thorn in the flesh (2 Cor. 12:7), the apostle prayed three times for its removal. In the process, Paul certainly must have searched his heart, asking the Lord, "Is there sin in my life? Is my attitude right?" When we encounter adversity, we would also do well to ask, *Am I in God's will, doing what He wants me to do?*

Perhaps you've done that and confessed any known sin, but the adversity persists. God deals not only with acts of transgression, but also with pre-programmed attitudes from youth. For many believers, it isn't a matter of overt sin or not loving the Lord, but something from the past that may be stunting spiritual growth.

To deal with core issues such as self-esteem, attitudes toward others, and even misguided opinions about God's capabilities, the Lord sends adversity intense enough to cause deeper examination than usual. He wants us to ask: *What fears, frustrations, and suffering from childhood are still affecting or driving me? Is an old attitude or grudge hurting me? Did a comment cause feelings of rejection or worthlessness?* An issue lying dormant for years may be hindering progress. Recognize in your adversity God's loving desire to help you reach your full spiritual potential.

Read 2 Corinthians 12:8-10 in your Bible. What was Paul's conclusion after this time of self-examination?

_____

How does that conclusion lead to living the

extraordinary life?_____

Some Reasons God Allows Adversity in Our Lives, Part 2

TO TEACH US TO HATE EVIL AS GOD DOES

Satan sells his sin program by promising pleasure, freedom, and fulfillment, but he doesn't tell you about the hidden costs. The truth is, "Whatever a man sows, this he will also reap" (Gal. 6:7).

People once trapped by drugs, alcohol, or sexual indulgence but now freed by God, will speak of their hatred for the sin. Because of the suffering, helplessness, and hopelessness they experienced, they have learned to despise the very thing they at one time desired. David agreed: "Before I was afflicted I went astray" (Ps. 119:67). If we could learn to anticipate sin's ongoing and future consequences, our lives would be far holier and healthier.

If you are a parent, you need to be honest with your children about failures. There is no such thing as a perfect father or mother, and pretending to have no faults is detrimental. Our children need to understand that God allows adversity for their protection. We should be frank about our weaknesses and clearly explain sin's effect, Satan's desires, and God's solution. Warn them by explaining how you responded to sin in your life and how they can avoid it in theirs. Your children will be blessed by your honesty.

To Cause Us to Reevaluate Our Priorities

We can become workaholics, exhausting ourselves and ignoring our children until it's too late. Or we can become so enamored of material things that we neglect the spiritual. So what happens? The Lord will do away with whatever dislocates our priorities.

God doesn't initiate family trials, but when He sees us neglecting His precious gifts or focusing in the wrong place, He may send a "breeze" of adversity as a reminder for us to check priorities. If the warning goes unheeded, however, a hurricane may be in the forecast. Then if we persist in ignoring the intensifying storm, it's as though He withdraws His hand and lets the adversity run its full course.

"The refining pot is for silver and the furnace for gold, but the LORD tests hearts" (Prov. 17:3, NASB).

Many fathers and mothers work hard to balance career and parenthood. There are inevitable points of conflict between the two, which can serve as cautionary breezes. But if priorities are misaligned, and moving up the corporate ladder becomes the exclusive goal, a whirlwind of adversity may be approaching.

What "breezes" might be reminding you to reevaluate your priorities?

_____

If you are facing a whirlwind in your family, how might God be calling you to realign your priorities?

_____

To Test Our Works

God already knew the outcome when He told Abraham to sacrifice his son. His purpose was not to discover what his response would be, but to show the patriarch where he was in his obedient walk of faith. When Abraham came off that mountain, not only did he know more about God than ever before but he also understood more about himself spiritually. Besides that, Isaac more than likely never forgot the experience! Children often remember things we do not expect—things far deeper than the externals. More than the sight of that pointed dagger, Isaac likely remembered that he had a father whose obedience to God knew no boundaries.

So when God sends adversity to test us, do our family members watch us buckle, or do they see us standing strong in faith, trusting the Lord to teach us, strengthen us, and bring good from the circumstance? Remember that our response carries a weighty influence for good or for evil in the lives of those who love us most.

Read 1 Peter 4:12-13 in your Bible. What are positive ways to respond to adversities?

_____

As you face hardship, keep in mind that its intensity will not exceed your capacity to bear it. God *never* sends adversity into your life to break your spirit or destroy you. If you respond improperly, you can destroy yourself, but God's purpose is always to bless, to strengthen, to encourage, and to bring you to the maximum of your potential.

Adversity touches every life. Instead of running from it, ask the Lord, "What are You trying to teach me?" While it's OK to tell Him you don't like it and you wish He'd take it away, I challenge you to add, "But don't quit, God, until You have finished."

Read 1 Peter 1:6-9, printed in the margin. What will be the end result when God finishes?

_____

God has something for us to learn through each trial. He never wastes our sorrows. He uses each one to draw us closer to Him. In 2 Corinthians, the apostle Paul wrote, "We are afflicted in every way, but not crushed; perplexed, but not despairing; persecuted, but not forsaken; struck down, but not destroyed" (4:8–9). True peace does not come as a result of eliminating sorrows and disappointments. It comes as a result of one thing, and that is an intimate relationship with the Lord Jesus Christ. He is where anxiety ends and peace begins.

Sincerely pray the prayer printed in the margin.

"In this you greatly rejoice, though now for a little while you may have had to suffer grief in all kinds of trials. These have come so that your faith—of greater worth than gold, which perishes even though refined by fire—may be proved genuine and may result in praise, glory and honor when Jesus Christ is revealed. Though you have not seen him, you love him; and even though you do not see him now, you believe in him and are filled with an inexpressible and glorious joy, for you are receiving the goal of your faith, the salvation of your souls" (1 Pet. 1:6-9, NIV).

Prayer:
Dear Heavenly Father, thank You for the hardships that You bring into my life. Please teach me through them, and show me how to accept them as Your work in my life. Amen.

To the Leader:

What's happening in the world or in participants' lives that might lead them to exclaim that the world is out of control? Prayerfully determine how, through your life and teaching, you can encourage learners that you are confident God is completely and sovereignly in control of everything.

Before the Session

Research gold at *http://www.nma.org/about_us/publications/pub_gold_uses.asp* or at *www.earthwormtunneling.com/gold.html* for answers to the questions in Step 1 option.

During the Session

1. Ask participants to identify individuals who have lived extraordinary lives while you record learners' responses on the board. Ask: *How many of these extraordinary people lived easy lives? Would you say their trials hindered or contributed to their extraordinary lives? Explain.* OR Inform the class they are going to review high school chemistry. Ask learners who recalls the symbol for gold. Then lead learners to discuss why gold is an extraordinary metal, the uses for gold, and the process by which gold is purified. Explore why gold must be refined in order to retain its extraordinary status.

2. Discuss the first activity of Day 1. Request participants follow along in their Bibles as a volunteer reads aloud Jeremiah 9:4-6. Ask if Jeremiah's description of his nation sounds familiar to your class participants and why. Request participants state from Jeremiah 9:7-9 what God was going to do and why. Ask learners to read verses 10-11 to discover the refining process God was going to use on His people. Ask: *Why does God allow such pain in the lives of His children?* Have learners read Jeremiah 9:12-16 to help answer that question.

3. Ask what statement became an anchor to Dr. Stanley's soul during times of trial. Request someone read aloud the definition of *sovereignty* in the margin of page 79. Discuss the second activity of Day 1. Acknowledge that we might think that if God's busy taking care of the universe, He surely doesn't have time for us. Read aloud Matthew 10:29-31 and assure participants God is sovereign over big and small things. Explore how God's sovereignty gives His children assurance and comfort when they are being refined by difficult circumstances. Use Dr. Stanley's comments from Day 1 to add to the discussion.

4. Read aloud the title for Day 2. Ask participants how that principle is true in sports and in education. Ask why God allows trials in the lives of His children. Invite volunteers to share how they have grown stronger through their trials. Use the activities in Day 2 to help explore the content of that day. Urge participants to determine ahead of time that they will stand firm in God's Word and His ways no matter what trials come their way.

5. Ask: *Who is immune from problems?* Contrast humanity's view of problems with God's view. Inquire: *No matter the source of our trials, whether they're from Satan, God, or our own bad choices, of what can we be assured? So what's more important than determining the source of our trials?* [Determining how we will respond to them.] Review some of the adversities Joseph faced by summarizing Genesis 37:17-28 and 39:7-20. Read aloud Genesis 39:21-23. Inquire: *Based on just these verses, how might we surmise Joseph responded to his adversities?* Discuss the final activity of Day 3.

6. Ask how adversities get our attention. Discuss the first activity of Day 4. Explore Saul's different options in responding to His God-given adversities and how we have the same options. Remind learners that our choice in how we respond to our adversities affects far more lives than we can imagine. Discuss how trials are actually reminders of God's love. Request a volunteer read aloud 2 Corinthians 12:7-10. Consider what Paul might have been asking God and himself during that time. Ask learners to identify "thorns" in their lives that might be preventing them from reaching their full spiritual potential. Urge them to stay the course through painful times of self-examination so they can weed out the things that are hindering their spiritual progress. Discuss the final activity of Day 4.

7. Explore why adversity in our lives might teach us to hate evil as God does. Ask participants if they agree or disagree that parents need to be honest with their children about their own failures. Discuss: *How frank about our sins and their consequences should we be with our children? At what age and for what purpose should we share this information?* Invite volunteers to share how adversity has led them to reevaluate their priorities. Ask: *Who is watching how we respond to adversities?* Discuss the second activity of Day 5. Explore how our positive responses positively influence our children. Request someone read aloud from the margin 1 Peter 1:6-9. Direct the class to identify the types of trials, the time frame, and the purpose of trials. Ask, *What can keep believers going when the trials seem unbearable?* Discuss the final activity of Day 5. Pray the closing prayer together.

Fight Your Battles On Your Knees; You'll Win Every Time

day One

Leaning to Pray the Bible Way

If I asked whether or not you knew how to pray, you would probably answer, "Sure I do! All Christians know how to pray!" However, if you seriously examined the track record of your answered prayers, you might not be so sure.

One of the simplest but most profound passages on prayer in all of the Bible is found in the Sermon on the Mount. In Matthew 7:7–11 Jesus emphasized an important principle about prayer. Dispelling the assumption that prayer simply "comes naturally" for Christians, He asserted that prayer is an intentional, learned activity for God's children. In this passage, the Lord was quite simply showing the disciples the three basic steps for an effective prayer life.

What are those three basic steps according to Matthew 7:7-11?

_____ _____ _____

Clearly Jesus had in mind that we are to become actively involved in the prayer process. Prayer is not a spectator sport!

Somebody may ask, "Does that mean anybody and everybody can ask, seek, knock, and find?" No, because the Sermon on the Mount is addressed to the followers of Christ. He was talking about His own children.

There is a vital element in prayer that most people overlook, which is steadfastness in prayer. We may not see anything happening, but a delay between our asking and our receiving doesn't mean that God refuses to answer our prayers.

Read Luke 18:1-8 in your Bible. Describe the two characters in the parable.

1. The judge_____

2. The widow_____

Why did Jesus tell His followers this parable?

_____

Why did Jesus place this emphasis on perseverance? Because He very often delays answering prayer requests.

Why does God delay? If He sees within us attitudes of rebellion, bitterness, or unforgiveness, or if He notices certain unhealthy habits in our lifestyles, God postpones the answer for His children. He cannot and will not do so until you are in a spiritual position to receive it.

A second reason for God's delay is that He is in the process of testing our sincerity in order to build into us a persistent spirit. If we are really earnest, we will not make our request known just once and then give up if it goes unanswered for a time. That is why God says to pray, and to keep on praying, asking, seeking, and knocking.

Third, God often delays answering prayer in order to build our faith. As you and I begin to ask, seek, and knock, something happens in our walk with God. When we talk to Him, we are building and nourishing our relationship with Him. We are getting to know Him—who He is and how He operates.

A fourth reason for God's delays is to develop patience within us as we endure in prayer until His timing is right. God's timing does not always match our own.

Would you say that prayer is a vital part of your daily schedule? ❑ Yes   ❑ No

I know countless Christians who become involved in so many activities that prayer begins to shift aside as they diligently go about serving the Lord in their own strength and wisdom. One of the primary reasons we do not pray is that we have busied ourselves with so many distractions that we don't have time for the truly important things.

We do not always like the answers that God gives. He did not promise to give us anything we request; instead, He promises in Matthew 7:11 that everything He gives is good for us.

The privilege of prayer is a heritage that belongs to every child of God, a potential that is beyond human understanding. It is a work of God's grace that He has given to each one of us. It is my prayer that you will not let that heritage be wasted in your life.

day Two

A Real Enemy

Every single one of us faces a war each day—we battle the Devil. Yet many people do not recognize the work of Satan; they mistake his assault for the struggles of everyday life.

An enemy always wants to be camouflaged and covered so he can walk in the shadows undetected. Satan loves for people to doubt his existence, but do not be deceived—he is very real. Jesus clearly recognized the reality of the Devil, who tempted Him in the wilderness (Matt. 4:1). And we know Paul believed the scriptural account of Satan's temptation in the garden (Gen. 3) because in 2 Corinthians 11:3 he referred to the serpent that deceived Eve.

Read the passages printed in the margin and complete the statement below.

Satan is a _____, a _____,

a _____ and a _____.

"You are of your father the devil, and you want to do the desires of your father. He was a murderer from the beginning, and does not stand in the truth because there is no truth in him. Whenever he speaks a lie, he speaks from his own nature, for he is a liar and the father of lies" (John 8:44, NASB).

" … so that no advantage would be taken of us by Satan, for we are not ignorant of his schemes" (2 Cor. 2:11, NASB).

"For this reason, when I could endure it no longer, I also sent to find out about your faith, for fear that the tempter might have tempted you, and our labor would be in vain" (1 Thess. 3:5, NASB).

Satan tries to convince us that he does not exist. He wants us to believe that all religions are the same and everybody will get to heaven by one way or another. That is the way he operates: it all sounds good, but it is a lie.

Our enemy is very deliberate in the way he approaches us. He appeals to our minds first. The downward spiral begins with our thoughts. Our bodies simply turn in the direction our minds are facing. We must deliberately take control of our thinking because the mind is the battleground where Satan confronts us. If we are to win the battle against Satan, we must bring our thoughts under the control of the Lord Jesus Christ.

Read 2 Corinthians 10:3-5 and Philippians 4:8 in your Bible. To bring our thoughts under Christ's control, what thoughts must believers

destroy? _____

nurture? _____

The battle for our salvation was won at the cross—the Devil knows he is a defeated foe, destined for eternity in hell. Since he cannot take a single child of God with him, he tries to destroy our witness instead. However, when we recognize Satan's deception and depend upon the strength of Jesus Christ to resist him, we can be confident of victory.

day Three

The Strength to Stand

Satan is a very powerful adversary. And he is after your testimony—he wants to ruin your witness and make you as ineffective as possible. Thus the Bible tells us to stand firm and resist the Devil (Eph. 6:11; Jas. 4:7).

Paul laid out the battle plan in the sixth chapter of Ephesians. First, we must identify the enemy (vv. 11–12); second, we are to dress in the full armor of God and stand firm (vv. 13–17). The next verse reveals the key to withstanding Satan's onslaughts—we must appropriate the strength of the living God.

"With all prayer and petition pray at all times in the Spirit, and with this in view, be on the alert with all perseverance and petition for all the saints" (Eph. 6:18, NASB).

According to Ephesians 6:18, printed in the margin, how do we get God's power into our lives to be unleashed in any and every circumstance?

_____

It is through prayer that the Lord releases His energy, divine power, and protection, enabling us to live a godly, holy, and peaceful life regardless of our circumstances. Only through prayer can we sense forewarnings of Satan's attacks, which can be aimed anywhere—finances, family, relationships, or health. The one thing Satan hates above all else is the believer who knows how to persist in prayer and claim the promises of God—the enemy has no defense against persevering prayer, which crushes his might and sends him running. On the other hand, when we do not pray, we set ourselves up for defeat.

Since our enemy knows the power of prayer, he will use distractions against us to get our minds focused on anything but prayer. He will do everything possible to keep us from spending time in communion with our Heavenly Father. Satan wants us too busy to talk to the One who knows everything, loves us always, and desires to defend us in any situation.

"Your understanding of Scripture will be in direct proportion to your prayers. The holiness and righteousness of your life are directly related to your prayers. Your fruitfulness and usefulness to almighty God are also proportional to your communication with the Father."
—Charles Stanley

Read Colossians 4:2 and 1 Peter 4:7 in your Bible. What adjectives should describe a believer's prayer life?

_____

If you are prayerless, if you don't cry out for His divine direction and guidance, and if you don't put on His armor by faith every day, the enemy is going to succeed. And more than likely, he will hit you where you do not expect him to because that is his battle strategy.

The importance of prayer cannot be overemphasized. Your understanding of Scripture will be in direct proportion to your prayers. The holiness and righteousness of your life are directly related to your prayers.

Your fruitfulness and usefulness to almighty God are also proportional to your communication with the Father. It is critical that you understand praying is not "Lord, bless me, bless him, bless her. Give me this; give me that." Serious praying is talking to your Heavenly Father, who listens and desires to answer. It is about humbling yourself and acknowledging not only your need but also His presence, His holiness, and His righteousness. The source of our strength is the living God, and His power is channeled into our lives primarily when we listen and talk with Him.

Understanding exactly what it takes to release God's awesome power, Paul wrote, "With all prayer and petition pray at all times in the Spirit" (Eph. 6:18). By "all prayer," he was referring to prayer in general, that is, requests, thanksgiving, praise, and intercession (prayer to God on behalf of others), all of which are important. Next, he used the word "petition," which speaks of a particular, singular request.

> "We are most vulnerable to satanic attacks when we are not praying. "—Charles Stanley

We are most vulnerable to satanic attacks when we are not praying. Satan arranges a sequence of events in your life and mine to defeat us. He wants to get you too busy, distracted, or negligent to pray because once you are prayerless, you will soon become concerned and worried—burdens will become heavier, and you will feel discouraged and weary. Eventually you will feel emotionally, spiritually, and physically weak. Then when you drop your guard, Satan will hit you. You simply cannot afford to be prayerless!

Read Luke 11:1, printed in the margin. In the margin. personalize the disciples' request of Jesus to reflect the desire of your own heart when it comes to prayer.

> "It happened that while Jesus was praying in a certain place, after He had finished, one of His disciples said to Him, 'Lord, teach us to pray just as John also taught his disciples'" (Luke 11:1, NASB).

day *Four*

Pray Without Ceasing

Read 1 Thessalonians 5:17 in your Bible. What short, but powerful, instruction did Paul give believers?

_____

ASSURANCES

How can we pray at all times? It means living in God-consciousness. Think in terms of a telephone. If you hang up, you have disconnected the call. "Praying without ceasing" means you do not hang up—you continuously stay on the line with God. That is how He intends for us to live. If I meet somebody I have been praying for and something good has happened in his life, I will say, "Thank You, God, for what You did for him." If I see evil going on, I will say, "God, I am trusting You to correct this situation." The truth is, we should be able to talk to the Father specifically all the time. "Praying always" means living in communion with the Father, in constant awareness of His presence.

The only way we can be strong enough to withstand the traps and counterfeits of the Devil is by having a relationship whereby God is always speaking to our hearts and we are always talking to Him in return. You and I cannot be discerning unless we are praying as we ought. So, when you're driving down the expressway, what are you thinking about? Why don't you talk to God? When you wash the dishes and clean your house, what are you thinking about? You can talk to the Father. Talk to Him about everything. Satan wants you to think there are times when you do not need God—since he hates it when you are on your knees, he will keep you too busy to pray.

Is your prayer life ❏ **Pitiful?** **OR** ❏ **Powerful?**

No one else can put on your spiritual armor for you. If you want God's best in your life, get on your knees. Divine, supernatural power is available if you will cry out to God and claim it by faith. Your prayers release God's power into your life and make it possible for you to stand firm against every onslaught of the Devil.

Read in your Bible Romans 8:38-39; 1 Corinthians 10:13; and 1 Peter 5:8-9.

In the margin on page 96, list the ASSURANCES you find in God's Word.

In the margin on page 97, list the CAUTIONS you find in God's Word.

The Armor of God

Although we do have a real enemy who seeks our destruction, we are not defenseless. In Ephesians 6:10-17, Paul told us to put on the armor of God when we battle our spiritual enemies.

As you read Ephesians 6:10-17 below, underline the armor you are to put on.

> Finally, be strong in the Lord and in the strength of His might. Put on the full armor of God, so that you will be able to stand firm against the schemes of the devil. For our struggle is not against flesh and blood, but against the rulers, against the powers, against the world forces of this darkness, against the spiritual forces of wickedness in the heavenly places. Therefore, take up the full armor of God, so that you will be able to resist in the evil day, and having done everything, to stand firm.
>
> Stand firm therefore, having girded your loins with truth, and having put on the breastplate of righteousness, and having shod your feet with the preparation of the gospel of peace; in addition to all, taking up the shield of faith with which you will be able to extinguish all the flaming arrows of the evil one. And take the helmet of salvation, and the sword of the Spirit, which is the word of God (Eph. 6:10–17).

Though at times—especially in our present age—it seems we are in the midst of a horrendous physical battle, the real war is against the powers of spiritual darkness. Satan's goal has not changed over the years. The enemy knows his ultimate destiny, yet he will never give up his evil intent against the kingdom of God until Christ banishes him to the eternal lake of fire (Rev. 20:10). The only way he can do damage to the kingdom of God now is by enticing God's beloved children to yield to sin, thus damaging their fellowship with the Lord.

Satan will try to discourage you by filling your mind with an array of doubt and confusion, but you do not have to believe him. The message of the gospel of Christ is given to you as a sure authority. God's Word provides all the details you need to know about Satan.

Read Ephesians 6:10-17 again and circle a phrase Paul used more than once.

Paul also admonished us to "stand firm"—a phrase that denotes extreme faith in the One who gives us life and strength. But the enemy of faith is pride—a sure road to spiritual defeat. In the ministry, I have seen many who have fallen because of pride—they have been undone by their refusal to humble themselves before God and accept His plan for their lives. This is one reason why it is tremendously important to put on the entire armor that God has given to us. The armor keeps us mindful of who is in control of our lives and who is our Advocate before the Father (1 John 2:1).

On our own, we cannot defeat or even resist the enemy. Only through the power of Jesus Christ do we have the ability to stand and claim what God has done through His Son. The victory took place at Calvary (Col. 2:13–15). However, if we demand Satan's forces to leave without using the name of Jesus Christ, we position ourselves for a prideful defeat. Pride also comes into play when we think we are in control of our lives: "God is opposed to the proud, but gives grace to the humble" (Jas. 4:6).

Make a habit of claiming the armor of God each morning before you leave your house—this is a conscious act of submitting your life to the Lord as your final authority. Acknowledging your need for Him is a sign not of weakness but of unshakable trust. When you place your faith in Jesus Christ, heaven is on your side.

Are you standing fully clothed in His armor, or do you rise in the morning, grab a cup of coffee, and run out the door? Do you think of Jesus throughout the day, hoping to make more time for Him in the evening, only to find other commitments taking His place?

Establish and commit yourself to time alone with God. Let the life of Jesus Christ be your example.

Read the Scriptures printed in the margin. Circle when Jesus prayed.

Even before His day began—which was much busier than ours—Christ rose to be alone with the Father. Your life may be stretched to the limit. God knows what you are facing, and He will help you make time to be with Him if that is truly your heart's desire.

Whatever transpires in your life, the wisest decision you will ever make is the decision to spend time with the Lord on a regular basis. This teaches you to recognize Satan's movement and prepares you for battle when the enemy approaches. Paul told the Ephesians they were in a war, but clothed in the armor of God, they were assured of victory.

"In the early morning, while it was still dark, Jesus got up, left the house, and went away to a secluded place, and was praying there" (Mark 1: 35, NASB).

"It was at this time that He went off to the mountain to pray, and He spent the whole night in prayer to God" (Luke 6:12, NASB).

Prayer:

Dear Heavenly Father, as I begin this day, I put on, in faith, the belt of truth—I ask You to guide me through the decisions of my day. I put on the breastplate of righteousness—guard my emotions and my heart, and cause me to be pure. I put on my spiritual boots and ask for courage to share the gospel with any who need to hear. I put on my helmet of salvation, asking You to bring to my mind all You have done for me through Your Son, Jesus Christ. Finally I pick up my sword of the Spirit and ask You to bring to my mind Scripture that I have read, helping me to apply it to my life. I want to bring glory to Your name. Amen.

Will you make a personal covenant to spend consistent daily time in prayer with God? If so, fill out the commitment form below.

I commit to spend at least _____ minutes each day in prayer at (specify a time and place)

_____

Signed: _____

NOTES

Before the Session

Do a Web search of *oxymorons* to obtain a list for Step 1, Option.

During the Session

1. Ask: *In your experience, is the Christian life more like a walk in the park, a climb up a steep mountain, or a fierce battle with occasional cease-fires? Explain. Is any Christian's life going to be battle free? Why or why not?* OR Challenge participants to come up with a list of oxymorons [phrases that are contradictions in terms, such as: awfully nice, jumbo shrimp; personal computer; peace force; working vacation; plastic glasses]. Write responses on a writing surface. Add "prayer warrior" to the list and ask why some people might think that would be an oxymoron. Inquire: *Is it? Why?* FOR EITHER OPTION: Request someone state the eighth principle for living the extraordinary life by reading the title for Week 8.

2. Ask: *If a vibrant prayer life is directly linked to living the extraordinary life, what percentage of Christians would you say are living extraordinarily? Why? Does prayer just come naturally or is it something we need to learn how to do?* Declare that we must learn to pray the biblical way. Complete the first activity of Day 1 to discover the three basic steps for an effective prayer life. Ask: *Are "ask, seek, knock" active or passive verbs? So what did Jesus intend for our prayer lives?* Explore how some Christians make prayer a spectator sport. Read aloud Matthew 7:7 from the *Holman Christian Standard Bible* to show that the verbs "ask, seek, knock" signify a continual action. Ask why Christians often overlook the continual, steadfast component of prayer. Discuss the second activity of Day 1. Lead participants to explore the reasons God may delay answering our prayers. Request participants identify the phrase from Luke 18:7 that signifies who has the privilege of coming to God with persistent prayer.

3. Request learners identify conflicts and wars that are occurring in the world. Ask what battle occurs much closer to home on a daily basis. [Our battle against Satan.] Ask: *Do all Christians recognize that they are fighting a spiritual battle every day? Why or why not?* Request someone

To the Leader:

Pray daily for your class participants by name. Pray for their spiritual growth and any specific needs you know about. Choose a Scripture to pray regularly for your class, perhaps Ephesians 1:15-19; 3:14-19; Philippians 1:9-11; or Colossians 1:9-12 would be appropriate.

read aloud 2 Corinthians 11:3,14. Ask why Satan tries to camouflage his nature and activities. Lead learners to discover the truth about Satan by completing the first activity of Day 2. Ask: *Why is knowing your enemy in any battle essential to victory? Over what part of our lives will Satan seek to gain control first? Why?* Discuss the second activity of Day 2.

4. Inquire: *We know Satan can't have our souls once we give them to Christ, so why is he still fighting us?* Ask what the Bible tells us to do in Ephesians 6:11 and James 4:7 and why it tells us to do that instead of "arm yourself and go fight him." Declare that the war was won at Calvary, as believers, we just need to stand firm against Satan. Request participants state from Ephesians 6:18 the key to unleashing God's strength against satanic attacks. Lead the class to determine why the Devil will do anything he can to keep believers from praying and what distractions he will use. Discuss the second activity of Day 3.

5. To discover another adjective that should describe a believer's prayer life complete the first activity of Day 4. Determine what it means to pray without ceasing. [Option: Physically demonstrate Dr. Stanley's telephone illustration.] Encourage the class to give specific illustrations of how a believer could pray without ceasing all day on his or her commute, throughout the work day, while running errands, and while caring for family.

6. Invite someone to read aloud Ephesians 6:10-13. Request participants state the nature of the battle believers fight daily. Inquire: *Why would we be more likely to win if we recognized our struggles are spiritual battles?* Request participants identify the spiritual armor God has provided for every believer. Work together to determine specific ways truth, right standing with God, readiness to share the gospel, faith, assurance of salvation, and the Word of God can protect believers against Satan's attacks. Ask how we can put on this spiritual armor [see the closing prayer in Day 5].

7. Ask: *According to the Scriptures in the margin of Day 5, where was prayer on Jesus' list of priorities? What should it say to us that prayer was vital to Jesus' earthly victories?* Urge participants to make prayer a daily priority in their loves.

8. Lead the group in praying together the prayer on page 99.

9. Offer an opportunity for learners to fill in the personal covenant at the end of the lesson.

The Bible Is the Sourcebook of Life

day One

What We Believe, Part 1

Our belief system governs our lifestyle and choices—it is the foundation from which we form our opinions and make decisions. For Christians, it is absolutely essential to know what we believe and why. Most people inherit their convictions from their parents and simply absorb those ideas without really investigating them. But to be certain our system of thinking is accurate, we must base it on the Word of God and not on habit, culture, or even family heritage. If our mental grid has been built on the truth of the Bible, then we can detect false doctrine and philosophy.

As you read Peter's words printed in the margin, underline two reasons it is essential a Christian's belief system is based solely on the Word of God.

Let's consider a list of absolute truths that should be a foundational part of your belief system.

THE BIBLE

The Bible is God's unfolding revelation of Himself. It is His Word to the human race, explaining His intervention in history and nature, and His arrival in this world as the God-man. In keeping with 2 Timothy 3:16, we refer to the Scriptures as the inspired Word of God, or as "Godbreathed," which means the Lord chose individuals to record what He spoke to them. Since He who gave the Word is more than capable of protecting it from error, the Bible we have today is as reliable as when it was originally recorded.

"Just as there will also be false teachers among you, who will secretly introduce destructive heresies, even denying the Master who bought them" (2 Pet. 2:1, NASB).

"But sanctify Christ as Lord in your hearts, always being ready to make a defense to everyone who asks you to give an account for the hope that is in you, yet with gentleness and reverence" (1 Pet. 3:15, NASB).

The Word of the living God was given to us so we might grow in our relationship to Him. This is our instruction book for life and the final authority for what we believe.

THE GODHEAD

Although the specific term *Trinity* is not found in Scripture, the truth of the triune God appears throughout the Bible. Our one God consists of God the Father, God the Son, and God the Holy Spirit. They are characterized by the same attributes, but each has a different function.

Jesus Himself indicated these three comprise the Godhead when He said: "I will ask the Father, and He will give you another Helper, that He may be with you forever; that is the Spirit of truth" (John 14:16–17). Later He admonished His disciples to baptize in the name of the Father, the Son, and the Holy Spirit (Matt. 28:19).

Our Heavenly Father is the eternal and absolutely holy Creator God. He has control over every single thing.

God the Son is Jesus Christ, who took upon Himself human flesh and walked among men. He came to earth for the specific purpose of dying on the cross—His death was the substitutionary payment in full for our sin-debt (1 Pet. 3:18).

Read Romans 8:34 in your Bible.
What is God the Son doing now? _____

God the Holy Spirit dwells within every believer from the moment of salvation. Through Him, we have our spiritual gift(s) and the empowerment to do the work God chooses for our lives. The Holy Spirit transforms the life of the believer and brings forth good things (Gal. 5:22–23).

SATAN

The Bible tells us that God created Satan and made him an important angel (Ezek. 28:12–15). Satan is real. He so desired to be like God that he rebelled against the Creator, who subsequently cast him and his co-conspirators to earth. Here he has chosen to set up a counterfeit kingdom so he may reign as the god of this world (2 Cor. 4:4). Satan uses deception and division to deceive believers; he also desires to keep unbelievers away from the saving grace of Jesus Christ, thereby destroying

"In whose case the god of this world has blinded the minds of the unbelieving so that they might not see the light of the gospel of the glory of Christ, who is the image of God" (2 Cor. 4:4, NASB).

them. He instigates pain, sorrow, and spiritual death, but he disguises his intentions—he tries to lure people by whispering to them about indulging themselves and doing what feels good now. Satan speaks only of the present, not the future. He never mentions consequences.

As Christians, we have no cause to fear Satan.

Read the following Scriptures in your Bible and state two reasons Christians don't need to fear Satan.

1 John 4:4: _____

Revelation 20:10: _____

First, we are under the protection of the Holy Spirit; nothing can happen to us that God does not allow, and we know that He permits only those circumstances—no matter how bad they seem—that He can turn for our good. Second, we have seen Satan's obituary where he is thrown into a lake of fire, eternally punished for his rebellion against almighty God.

day *Two*

What We Believe, Part 2

MAN

God created man in His image to love us and fellowship with us. We are also privileged to glorify and serve Him. But when Adam and Eve disobeyed God, man's relationship to the Creator changed. At the same time, man's very nature became corrupt so that each of us is born with our will inclined away from God. Consequently we are separated from God.

No man can earn God's forgiveness or acceptance. Whatever "goodness" we have and whatever works we perform, they amount to nothing more than "filthy rags," in terms of meriting salvation (Isa. 64:6, NIV). But redemption works in our lives to change our nature and bend it back toward God.

Read Isaiah 53:4-6 in your Bible. In the margin, note what you learn about humanity's nature.

SALVATION

The simplest definition of *salvation* is "the gift of God's grace, whereby He provides forgiveness for our sins." Throughout the Old Testament, God's faithful people brought animal sacrifices to His altar in order to atone for their sins. These blood offerings foreshadowed the once-and-for-all sacrifice that was to come. Jesus Christ, whom John the Baptist rightly called the Lamb of God, died on a cross as a substitute for us. Thus our sin-debt was paid in absolute fullness. Now we are sealed in the Holy Spirit and eternally secure.

Salvation is by grace through faith in Jesus Christ; it is not something we receive based on our behavior. People who are saved do good works as an extension of their changed nature (Eph. 2:8–10). However, God gave mankind free will—we have a choice to receive the gift of grace or to reject Jesus Christ. No matter what you believe to be true about God or how good you try to be, there is no salvation for you if you reject the Son of God. The Lord said, "I am the way, and the truth, and the life; no one comes to the Father but through Me" (John 14:6).

"In Him, you also, after listening to the message of truth, the gospel of your salvation—having also believed, you were sealed in Him with the Holy Spirit of promise, who is given as a pledge of our inheritance, with a view to the redemption of God's own possession, to the praise of His glory" (Eph. 1:13-14, NASB).

THE CHURCH

The church is the whole body of Christ—believers from every part of the globe. It has nothing to do with being Baptist, Methodist, Presbyterian, or part of any denomination. If you have trusted Jesus Christ as your personal Savior, you are in the body of Christ, and God is your Heavenly Father.

Read the Scriptures listed below in your Bible and indicate responsibilities members of Christ's body have toward one another.

Galatians 6:2,10: _____

Ephesians 6:18: _____

Hebrews 10:24-25: _____

1 Peter 4:8: _____

As followers of Jesus, we are to express love for one another—encouraging, helping, and praying for fellow Christians. Our conduct should be in keeping with the One we call Lord and Master of our lives.

We meet in local groups to serve the Lord. The clear work of the church is to reach out and bring people to a saving knowledge of Jesus Christ. In addition, we instruct believers so all may grow in relationship to God. He has commanded us to "go therefore and make disciples of all the nations, baptizing them in the name of the Father and the Son and the Holy Spirit, teaching them to observe all that I commanded you" (Matt. 28:19–20).

Within the church, we practice two scriptural ordinances—baptism and the Lord's Supper. Baptism by immersion is a picture of what happens to every single person who is saved: We have put to death the old life and have risen to walk in the fullness and power of the Holy Spirit. Our character, conversation, and conduct are different because we are born again. Baptism does not save us; rather, it is an expression of obedience to Jesus' call that we be baptized in the name of the Father, the Son, and the Holy Spirit (Matt. 28:19).

Likewise, through the Lord's Supper, we rejoice in the blood of the new covenant between God and His children. When we receive the elements representing Jesus' body and blood, it is a time to celebrate our forgiveness. Even more, we celebrate His resurrection and the awesome anticipation of His return.

Every one of these issues is a vital part of the Christian's belief system, and they are all found in one place—the Word of God. If we know what it says, we will know what we must believe to live for His glory.

day Three

Practical Steps to Help You Acquire Spiritual Discernment

All genuine spiritual discernment comes from the Holy Spirit. It may come through another person or a Scripture reading, but the Holy Spirit makes it possible for you to hear the message as God speaks it.

Read John 14:26 and 16:13, printed in the margin, and complete the statement below.

Some of the Holy Spirit's vital roles in my life are to . . .

_____

"But the Helper, the Holy Spirit, whom the Father will send in My name, He will teach you all things, and bring to your remembrance all that I said to you" (John 14:26, NASB).

Here are a few practical steps that will help you listen to the Holy Spirit and acquire the spiritual discernment necessary to make wise decisions:

CLEAR THE PATHWAY OF YOUR MIND

To hear God's voice, you must clear your life of all known unconfessed sin. You must be willing to ask the Lord to forgive you and cleanse your life. You must also clear your thinking of your personal desires. This does not mean that you empty your mind and stop thinking or having desires. It means that you must be willing to honestly open yourself to God's will for your life.

EXERCISE PATIENCE

One key to finding spiritual discernment is patience. You must be willing to wait until God shows you His way. Patience is a sure sign of spiritual maturity. James 1:4 states, "Let patience have its perfect work, that you may be perfect and complete, lacking nothing" (NKJV).

"But when He, the Spirit of truth, comes, He will guide you into all the truth; for He will not speak on His own initiative, but whatever He hears, He will speak; and He will disclose to you what is to come" (John 16:13, NASB).

RESIST PRESSURE

Pressure is one of your greatest enemies when you seek to discern God's will. There are two types of pressure: external (the pressure of other people's opinions or imposed time limits) and internal (the pressure of your spirit). When you make a decision based upon perceived pressure, rather than clear guidance and direction from God, you risk doing the wrong thing.

PERSIST IN PRAYER

The key in this area is not simply praying but persisting in prayer. That is, throughout the day—in the morning, in the afternoon, and in the evening—pray consistently and passionately (1 Thess. 5:17). Prayer is God's way of preparing you for an answer. As you begin to pray, He begins to show you things in your life, such as attitudes or motives, that need to be examined.

LEAN ON GOD'S PROMISES

When you face a major decision, turn to the Word of God and ask Him to show you a promise. The Scriptures are full of God's promises, which are evidence of His divine guidance. God said, "I will instruct you and teach you in the way which you should go; I will counsel you with My eye upon you" (Ps. 32:8). The author of Proverbs wrote, "Trust in the LORD with all your heart and do not lean on your own understanding. In all your ways acknowledge Him, and He will make your paths straight" (3:5–6). These are specific promises that God truly desires to give you guidance and direction for your life.

WAIT FOR PEACE

Colossians 3:15 urges you to "let the peace of Christ rule in your heart." Regardless of the pressure you may feel, wait for peace. You may seek confirmation from others, but be careful that their confirmation is in keeping with what God has said in His Word. Perfect peace is God's verdict when you have His mind and His way. Don't budge until you get God's peace. This is the final confirmation of a wise decision.

Read Isaiah 26:3-4 and John 14:1,27 in your Bible.

What kind of peace must we seek? _____

How do we obtain that kind of peace? _____

Every believer can walk in confidence and assurance that he is walking in God's will. If you clear your conscience, wait patiently, resist pressure, persist in prayer, lean on His promises, and wait for His peace, He will speak truth to your heart and mind. Isaiah 30:21 states, "Your ears will hear a word behind you, 'This is the way, walk in it,' whenever you turn to the right or to the left.' "

How to Gain God's Wisdom

The writer of Proverbs reminded us that "wisdom is supreme; therefore get wisdom. Though it cost all you have, get understanding" (Prov. 4:7, NIV).

How do we gain the wisdom of God for our lives?

We gain wisdom when we seek God. We must believe that if we go to God with even the smallest detail, He will hear our prayer and answer it. This is exactly what He does. He will answer us in one of three ways: yes, no, or wait.

We gain wisdom when we learn to meditate on God's Word.

According to Psalm 19:7-8, printed in the margin, why would intense focusing on God's Word result in wisdom?

_____

"The law of the LORD is perfect, restoring the soul; The testimony of the LORD is sure, making wise the simple. The precepts of the LORD are right, rejoicing the heart; The commandment of the LORD is pure, enlightening the eyes" (Ps. 19:7-8, NASB).

If we really want to receive a blessing, we must take our requests to God through prayer and then seek His guidance through His Word. God never will contradict His Word. Scripture provides a solution for every problem or decision we face. Scripture is not out of date. Therefore, we can trust the Word of God to provide the guidance we need.

We gain wisdom when we learn to obey the principles of Scripture. We must learn to obey God and learn to follow the pathway God places before us. This means that we submit our human desires to God, which speaks volumes of our love for the Lord.

Do you love the Lord so much that you are willing to release all that you have so God can live His life through you? ❑ **Absolutely** ❑ **No**
❑ **I really want to get to that point.**

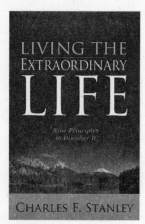

We gain wisdom as a result of prayer. In times of prayer, we learn to humble our hearts before God. We also learn to be quiet and listen for God's voice through the Holy Spirit. When it comes, our spirits hear God's Word and immediately respond with gladness and thanksgiving.

We gain wisdom by observing how God works in our world. Though our lives may be touched by death, sin, and sorrow, God is Lord over all, and He will bring purpose out of each event.

We gain wisdom through wise counsel. Talk your problems over with trusted Christian friends, a counselor, or a pastor. Once they have given you their view or counsel, take this to God in prayer. If what they have told you is from God, it will not violate Scripture or any principle of God's Word.

We gain wisdom when we associate with wise people. There are people who may seek to speak a "word of knowledge" to us. What they have to say may or may not be on target with God's plan for our lives. You can avoid disappointment and feelings of discouragement when you ask God to sift what they have said to you through His infinite grid of wisdom, God's Word.

Whom do you consider to be a wise person? _____

Indicate in the margin what makes that person wise in your opinion.

day *Five*

Requirements for Wisdom

We seek wisdom to please God and to gain His perspective on our lives and individual situations. Here are the requirements for wisdom:

Have a strong determination to walk wisely. Our motivation for wisdom must begin and end with a love for God—we want to please Him.

Meditate on God's Word. God instructed Joshua to meditate on His Word day and night. The psalmist told us to hide the Word of God in our hearts (Ps. 119:11).

Learn to be sensitive to the prompting of the Holy Spirit. The amazing part of seeking the wisdom of God is that we can learn to hear His voice. When the prophet Elijah lost his perspective, God spoke to him. However, the Lord's voice did not come to His prophet through an earthquake or storm. It came in the form of a still, quiet voice. When we are still—in our thoughts and emotions—God will speak to our hearts the way He did to Elijah. He commands us to "be still, and know that I am God" (Ps. 46:10, NKJV).

Believe God is the Source of wisdom. Faith and trust are necessary in gaining the wisdom of God. Human reasoning will fail you.

Read James 1:5-6, printed in the margin. Circle the action you must take to acquire wisdom. Underline the attitude that must under gird the action. Finally, draw a star over the words that describe how God will give you wisdom.

Have courage to obey God. Obedience reveals our true desire for wisdom. If we seek to obey God, then we are on the road to true wisdom. There will be times when God will require us to go forward without knowing all that is ahead. Blessings come to those who obey God. Therefore, we should be courageous and go forward by faith, trusting God to make our pathways safe.

Persevere. When you can say, "I know that I am doing the right thing. Therefore, I am going to keep my focus and continue on," then you are learning perseverance. The wisdom of God will come to you.

Becoming the extraordinary masterpiece God created you to be is a lifelong process. Read the Bible's promises below and state how each encourages you to keep applying these nine principles for an extraordinary life.

Philippians 1:6: _____

1 Thessalonians 5:23-24: _____

"But if any of you lacks wisdom, let him ask of God, who gives to all generously and without reproach, and it will be given to him. But he must ask in faith without any doubting, for the one who doubts is like the surf of the sea, driven and tossed by the wind" (Jas. 1:5-6, NASB).

Prayer:
Dear Heavenly Father, thank You for Your Word that is a lamp to our feet and a light to our path. Please give me a hunger to read it more faithfully and a mind to understand it more clearly. Please show me how to apply Your principles to my life. Amen.

leader Guide

To the Leader:

Contact, either by phone, card, e-mail or personal visit, participants who have not been present in Bible Study for a few weeks. Make sure they have a copy of this issue of *MasterWork* and urge them to attend next week as you begin the new study of *The Five Languages of Apology* by Gary Chapman and Jennifer Thomas.

Before the Session

Create a display of strainers or sieves, such as a colander, flour sifter, tea strainer, and window screen (for Step 1, Option).

During the Session

1. Ask learners if they agree or disagree with the saying, "You are what you eat" and why. Then ask if they agree or disagree that "You are what you believe" and why. OR Draw attention to the display of strainers. Ask what the items have in common. [They separate undesired elements from desired elements or they screen out unwanted things.] Determine how a person's belief system is like a mental strainer. [All outside elements must pass through a person's belief system, some get past, unwanted elements get strained out.] FOR EITHER OPTION: Evaluate what often determines a person's belief system. State that the ninth principle of living the extraordinary life is that Christians are to base their system of thinking, believing, and acting on the Word of God.

2. Explore why it is essential for Christians to know what they believe. [See the first activity of Day 1.] Ask what Christians must believe about the Bible. Request two volunteers read aloud 2 Timothy 3:16 and 2 Peter 1:20-21. Ask why those truths about God's Word must be foundational for everything else Christians believe. Ask what every believer must believe about the Godhead. Request participants examine Genesis 1:2,26 and state how the Trinity was evident even at the beginning of creation. [You may want to take adults to John 1:1-3 to further understand that God the Son was present at creation.] Ask why a belief about Satan must be a foundational truth Christians must grasp. [We need to know who our enemy is so we'll know how to fight him.] Discuss the final activity of Day 1.

3. Declare that a foundational part of every Christian's belief system should be an accurate knowledge of his or her own human nature. Request participants state absolute truths about humanity. Discuss the first activity of Day 2. Guide the class to identify from Isaiah 53:4-6 truths about God and salvation. Request participants state what they learn

about salvation from Ephesians 1:13-14, printed in the margin of Day 2. Using this passage, trace the role of each member of the Trinity in salvation. Instruct one-third of the class to read Ephesians 1:1-6, another third of the class to read Ephesians 1:7-14, and the final third of the class to read Ephesians 1:15-19. Invite volunteers from each group to share privileges of being saved and belonging to Christ's church. Acknowledge that along with privilege comes responsibility. Complete the second activity of Day 2. Help the group determine other responsibilities that come with belonging to Christ's body. Read aloud the final paragraph of Day 2. Remind learners that living the extraordinary life is dependent on knowing and believing God's Word.

4. Ask participants if they agree or disagree with the statement that life is made up of one decision after another. Inquire: *What are some major/ minor decisions we're all facing? Which require godly discernment?* Read aloud 1 John 5:14 and ask what believers can know for certain as they face decisions. Declare that God wants to show us His will and His plan and purpose. Explore how that was true in the life of Abraham (Gen. 12:1), Gideon (Judg. 6:14,36-40), and Paul (Acts 16:6-10). Remark that God continues to speak to His people today, particularly through Scripture. Discuss the first activity of Day 3. Use Dr. Stanley's comments and the activities in Day 3 to discover practical steps for spiritual discernment.

5. Assert that we live our lives one of two ways—wisely or unwisely. Only one way leads to extraordinary living, so we need to learn how to gain God's wisdom. Organize the class into two groups. Instruct Group 1 to read Proverbs 2:1-9 and 4:1-9 and identify verses that coincide with Dr. Stanley's suggestions for gaining God's wisdom in Day 4. Ask them to become familiar enough with Day 4 so they can present the contents to the entire class. Instruct Group 2 to identify verses from the same proverbs that support the requirements for wisdom in Day 5 and be prepared to present that day's material to the whole class. Allow time for investigation, reports, and discussion.

6. To review this entire study, ask the class to define extraordinary living. [See the Introduction on p. 5.] Review the nine principles [each week's title] and discuss how each contributes to living the extraordinary life. Discuss the final activity in Day 5.

7. Pray together the closing prayer on page 111.

Gary Chapman, internationally respected marriage and family expert, is also senior associate pastor at Calvary Baptist Church in Winston-Salem, North Carolina. Dr. Chapman has authored more than 20 books, including *Now You're Speaking My Language* and *The Love Languages of God.*

Jennifer Thomas is a psychologist and counselor in Winston-Salem, North Carolina. Dr. Thomas is a member of the American Association of Christian Counselors. She and husband, J.T., have three children.

JOE BECKLER wrote the personal learning activities and teaching plans for this study. A church planter in Colorado, Joe holds a Master of Divinity degree from New Orleans Baptist Theological Seminary.

ABOUT THIS STUDY

1. What do you think the word *apology* means?

_____

2. What do you look for in an apology when you have been wronged?

_____

3. When you apologize to someone, what do you think is the most important part of the apology?

_____

The Five Languages of Apology

In a perfect world, there would be no need for apologies. But because the world is imperfect, we cannot survive without them. The person who refuses to recognize the need for an apology will have a life filled with broken relationships—marriage, parenting, dating, and vocational. Something within us cries out for reconciliation when wrong doing has fractured a relationship.

When we apologize, we accept responsibility for our behavior, seeking to make amends with the person who was offended. What most people are looking for in an apology is sincerity, but how do you determine sincerity? The evidence of sincerity differs from person to person.

What our research has clearly revealed is that when it comes to apologizing, people indeed speak different languages. We have discovered five fundamental aspects of an apology. We call them the five languages of apology. Each of them is important. Yet, for most people, one or two of these speak more deeply of sincerity than the others. The key to good relationships is learning the apology language of the other person and being willing to speak it.

The good news is that the art of apology can be learned. The wonderful thing about being human is that we are capable of change, especially when we reach out for God's help. Our study over the next four weeks will introduce you to the five languages of apology and the power they have to change your relationships.

Gary Chapman and *Jennifer Thomas*

Brand X Pictures/
Jupiterimages Unlimited

Expressing Regret and Accepting Responsibility

day One

Language 1: Expressing Regret

Expressing Regret

"I am sorry."

"Regret focuses on
what you did or failed to
do and how it affected
the other person."

—Gary Chapman

Apology is birthed in the womb of regret. Regret focuses on what you did or failed to do and how it affected the other person. Offended people are experiencing painful emotions, and they want you to feel some of their pain. They want some evidence that you realize how deeply you have hurt them. For some people, this is the one thing they listen for in an apology. Without the expression of regret, they do not sense that the apology is adequate or sincere.

> **David understood how to express regret.**
> **Read Psalm 51. Write in the margin words and phrases**
> **from this psalm that express David's feelings of regret.**

SAYING THE MAGIC WORDS

The first language of apology is *expressing regret*. Most commonly spoken with the words "I am sorry," expressing regret is the emotional aspect of an apology. It is expressing to the offended person your own sense of guilt, shame, and pain that your behavior has hurt him deeply.

The absence of the words "I'm sorry" stands out to some like a very sore thumb. Quite often offenders will not realize that they have left out some "magic words," but you can be assured that the listener is scanning the silence for those missing words.

Karen has been married to her husband, Jim, for twenty-seven years. When I asked her, "What do you look for in an apology when Jim has wronged you?" her immediate response was, "Most of all I want him to understand how he hurt me and why. I want him to see things from my perspective. I expect to hear him say, 'I apologize. I am really sorry.' It helps if he gives an explanation of how his actions have hurt me. That way, I know he understands. If it is something really bad, I expect abject misery and want him to really be sad about the pain he caused me."

WHAT DOES YOUR BODY SAY?

It is important that our body language agree with the words we are saying if we expect the offended person to sense our sincerity. Robert and Katie have been married for seven years. When I asked him, "How do you know that Katie is sincere when she apologizes?" his answer was, "Eye contact. If she looks me in the eye and says 'I'm sorry,' I know she's sincere. If she says 'I'm sorry' while passing through the room, I know she's hiding something. A hug and a kiss after the apology also let me know that she's sincere."

Robert is illustrating the reality that sometimes our body language speaks louder than our spoken language. This is especially true when the two contradict each other. For example, one wife said, "When he screams at me, 'I said I'm sorry,' but his eyes are glaring and his hands are shaking, it's like he's trying to make me forgive him. It seems to me he is more concerned about moving on and forgetting it than truly apologizing. It's like my hurt doesn't matter—let's just get on with life."

List in the margin examples of body language that reflect sincere expression of regret.

SORRY FOR WHAT?

An apology has more impact when it's specific. LuAnn captured this idea when she said, "I expect the apologizer to say 'I'm sorry for ____' and then be specific about what he is sorry about." When we're specific, we communicate to the offended person that we truly understand how much we have hurt him or her. Specificity places the focus on our action and how it affected the other person.

On the next page, read the details of how Dr. Thomas would express regret (see the margin). Think of a time

Give the details:

If I stood someone up for a movie, I wouldn't just say, "I'm sorry I didn't make it." It would mean more to the person if I could list all the ways my action affected her. I would say, "I know that you left home on time. You made it here during rush-hour. You had to wait and were concerned about my well-being. I know you like to see the entire picture. You have a right to be angry and upset. I want you to know that I am sincerely sorry for my irresponsibility."

you apologized. Write a more specific apology than you might have given at the time.

_____

_____

Read Luke 18:9-14. Note in the margin how this parable relates to our need to specifically express what we are sorry for.

Getting It Right

Joanne is a twenty-seven-year-old single who has been in a committed dating relationship for three years. She said, "Anytime an apology is followed by an excuse for the offense, the excuse cancels out the apology in my mind. Just own up that, intentionally or not, you hurt me or didn't meet my expectations. Don't apologize and then make excuses for your offense. Leave it at the apology."

AVOIDING THE "BUT ..."

Sincere regret needs to stand alone. It should not be followed with "But...." Numerous individuals in our research made statements similar to this one, "She apologizes, then blames her actions on something I did to provoke her. Blaming me does little to make the apology sincere." Anytime we verbally shift the blame to the other person, we have moved from an apology to an attack. Attacks never lead to forgiveness and reconciliation.

Reread Psalm 51. How did David model regret without saying "but ..."?

_____

On a scale of 1 to 10 (1 being rarely and 10 being always), how often do you try to blame or excuse-away your mistakes? _____

APOLOGIES THAT DO NOT MANIPULATE

Good relationships are fostered by expressing regret even when we did not intend to hurt someone. If I bump into someone getting out of an elevator, I say "I'm sorry," not because I intentionally bumped him but because I identify with his inconvenience or irritation with my unintentional bump. The same principle is true in close relationships. You may not realize that your behavior has upset your spouse, but when it becomes apparent, then you can say, "I'm sorry that my behavior caused you so much pain. I didn't intend to hurt you."

An expression of sincere regret should not manipulate the other person into reciprocating. Insincerity is also communicated when we say "I'm sorry" simply to get the other person to stop confronting us with the issue. Rhonda sensed this when she said, "Early in our marriage, my husband did something really damaging. He absolutely refused to be sorry or repent. Then eventually he said that he was sorry, but it was only to get me off his back. His actions spoke more loudly than his words, indicating: 'Drop it! I want to get out of this trap.' He didn't see that what he had done was wrong and hurt me deeply."

> "Good relationships are fostered by expressing regret even when we did not intend to hurt someone."
>
> —Gary Chapman

Look again at Psalm 51:16-17. Note in the margin how these verses relate to our sincerity in apologizing.

"I HOPE YOU CAN FORGIVE ME"

Writing a letter of apology may help to underscore your sincerity. To put your apology in writing may give it more emotional weight, because your spouse or friend can read it again and again. The process of writing may also help you clarify your regrets and verbalize them in a positive way.

Olivia received a letter from her husband Jim apologizing for being late on a difficult night when she had called for help with the children. Jim's expression of regret got through to Olivia. She sensed his sincerity and was willing to forgive him. Olivia wrote at the bottom of the page, "Forgiven on 1/20/05."

STATEMENTS
OF REGRET

❏ I know now that I hurt you very deeply. That causes me immense pain. I am truly sorry for what I did.

❏ I feel really bad that I disappointed you. I should have been more thoughtful. I'm sorry that I caused you so much pain.

❏ At the time, obviously I was not thinking very well. I never intended to hurt you, but now I can see that my words were way out of line. I'm sorry that I was so insensitive.

❏ You were promised a service that we have not provided. I am sorry that our company clearly dropped the ball this time.

The language of regret focuses on the other person's pain and your behavior and how the two are related. It is this identification with the other person's pain that stimulates a willingness to forgive. Without it, the offended one will hear your words, but they will appear empty. When the other person does hear your words, he or she is fully willing to forgive. Without them, forgiveness becomes difficult.

LEARNING THE LANGUAGE

Vicky, age twenty-six and single, says, "I want an apology that comes from the heart, that is truly sorry for the action that caused my hurt. In other words, I want the person to feel bad for making me feel bad."

Ted adds, "[It's a genuine apology] when she expresses true feelings of regret, expresses understanding of my feelings and acts like she is sorry that she hurt me."

For these and others, the apology language of expressing regret is extremely important in the process of healing and restoration. If you are willing to express regret, there are some statements to help you do so.

Read the statements of regret printed in the margin. Check two statements that you could use in relationship situations this week.

day *Three*

Language 2: Accepting Responsibility

For many individuals, hearing the words "I was wrong" is what communicates an apology. Without these or similar words that accept responsibility for one's wrong behavior, they will not sense that the other person has sincerely apologized. The second language of apology is *accepting responsibility*.

Accepting Responsibility

"I was wrong."

Read the scenarios printed in the margin of the next page. Underline how Larry, Jane, and Shawn each

attempted to avoid feeling at fault. Why do you suppose accepting responsibility is such a hard thing for us to embrace?

_____

"IT'S NOT MY FAULT"

Larry, Jane, and Shawn all felt a tug of guilt but also felt their excuses covered the need to apologize. Why is it so difficult for some of us to say, "I was wrong"? Often our reluctance to admit wrongdoing is tied to our sense of self-worth. To admit that we are wrong is perceived as weakness. We may reason, *Only losers confess. Intelligent people try to show that their actions were justified.*

The seeds of a self-justifying tendency are often planted in childhood. Subconsciously, the child, overly punished or shamed for minor offenses, makes the emotional link between wrong behavior and low self-worth.

Mature adults learn how to break the harmful patterns of childhood and accept responsibility for their own failures. The immature adult is forever rationalizing his own bad behavior. Such rationalization often takes the form of blaming others. We may admit that what we did or said was not the best, but our behavior was provoked by the other person's irresponsible actions.

Read 2 Samuel 12:1-15. How did David react to being confronted with his fault? How do you typically react to being confronted with your faults?

_____

_____

Romans 3:23 reads, "For all have sinned and fall short of the glory of God." How does this truth make it easier for us to admit our fault?

_____

As a boss, Larry usually stayed calm, but today he ran out of patience. He spoke cutting words in anger. Afterward, he felt bad but told himself, "What I said was true. The guy needs to shape up and know I'm not a pushover."

Jane once again arrived halfway through a neighborhood meeting. She was confused about the meeting time. Having just returned from a cross-country trip, she didn't know what day it was, much less the time of the day. Meanwhile, the others at the meeting felt she owed them an apology for again showing up late.

Shawn was in pain after a medical procedure. He unkindly swatted away Mom's attempts to make him comfortable. Shawn knew his action was degrading, but he reasoned, "Medicine can make anyone act crazy. Mom should understand."

The good news is that as adults we can understand these negative emotional patterns and yet not be imprisoned by them. The reality is that all of us are sinners; there are no perfect adults.

"I WAS WRONG"

At the heart of accepting responsibility for one's behavior is the willingness to admit wrongdoing. Dr. Spencer Johnson says, "Few things are more powerful than having the common sense, wisdom, and strength to admit when you've made a mistake and to set things right."[1] Learning to say "I was wrong" is a major step toward becoming a responsible and successful adult.

In the margin, write the name of a person in your life to whom you need to admit that you were wrong.

Record what you find the hardest to verbalize to that person.

Learning to Admit Mistakes

Joy and Rich were in my office after five years of marriage. In Joy's words: "Really, our lives are wonderful. The only problem is, Rich is never willing to apologize. When he gets upset because things don't go his way, he lashes out at me in anger. Instead of apologizing, he blames me for his anger. Even the few times he has said 'I'm sorry,' he adds, 'But if you had not provoked me, I would not have gotten angry.' I know that I am not a perfect wife, but I'm willing to admit when I do wrong. Rich never admits it."

When I turned to Rich, he said, "I don't think it is right to apologize for something when it is not your fault. I do get mad, but it's because she puts me down and makes me feel like I'm not a good father." It was obvious to me that Joy's comments were striking at Rich's self-esteem. He wanted to be a good father, and her comments suggested that he was a failure. His way of expressing his hurt was to lash out with angry words.

The fact is both Joy and Rich needed to apologize. The problem was that neither thought that he or she had done anything wrong. When a relationship is fractured by hurt and anger, an apology is always in order. Rich was hurt by the condemning message that he heard from Joy. Joy was hurt by the words that Rich hurled back at her. Neither of them intended to hurt the other. Yet both were guilty of treating each other unkindly.

Rich had grown up with an unhealthy family model. It was easy to understand why he responded the way he did to Joy. But to accept that behavior as appropriate was to destroy the very thing he wanted— an intimate marriage. I tried to help Rich see the difference between *understanding* why we do what we do and *accepting* what we do.

How has your family background shaped your patterns of communication and conflict resolution?

_____

_____

THE AGREE/DISAGREE APPROACH

I challenged Rich to a new approach. I call it "agree/disagree." I agree that I have a right to feel hurt, angry, disappointed, and frustrated or whatever else I may be feeling. On the other hand, I disagree that because of the feelings I am experiencing, I have the right to hurt someone else with my words or behavior. To hurt my spouse because my spouse has hurt me is like declaring civil war. Therefore, I will seek to express my emotions in a way that will not be hurtful to my spouse but will hold potential for reconciliation. We worked together on a statement to do that.

Read Rich's statement printed in the margin. Underline phrases that "hold potential for reconciliation."

Then I said, "I've worked with people long enough to know that simply having a new plan will not necessarily stop the old patterns. Chances are you will revert to your old pattern of lashing out. It's not what you want to

"Honey, I love you and Ethan very much. I want more than anything to be a good husband and father. Maybe I want it even more because I didn't have a close relationship with my dad, and I saw my folks fight each other all the time. Therefore, I want to share something with you that hurts me very deeply, and I want to ask you to help me find a solution. When I heard you say last night, 'If you don't spend more time with Ethan, he's going to grow up and not know who you are,' I felt a dagger pierce my heart. In fact, I cried because that's the last thing in the world I want. So can you help me work on my schedule so I can have meaningful time with Ethan and yet be able to work and meet our financial needs?"

"Last night, I lost my temper. I yelled at you and said some pretty nasty things. I was wrong to do that. It was not tender, it was not loving, and it was not kind. I know I hurt you very much and I'm sorry, because I don't want to hurt you. And I want to ask you to forgive me. I know I was wrong."

do, but you will do it before you think. This is when an apology is necessary. I think you will agree that yelling at one's wife is not kind, loving, tender, or positive." Rich was nodding his head. "Therefore, it is wrong."

Read the apology that Rich learned to say, found in the margin. Circle the words or phrases that show that he accepted responsibility for his actions.

LEARNING NEW WAYS TO RESPOND

Joy found it almost impossible to understand how a man could rage at his wife in anger if he really loved her. It is true that perfect love would never hurt the one loved. But none of us is capable of perfect love for one simple reason. Romans 3:23 says, "For all have sinned and fall short of the glory of God." Even those who say they are Christians are still capable of sinning. That is why we must learn to confess our sins to God and to the person we've sinned against.

"If we say, 'We have no sin,' we are deceiving ourselves, and the truth is not in us. If we confess our sins, He is faithful and righteous to forgive us our sins and to cleanse us from all unrighteousness. If we say, 'We have not sinned,' we make Him a liar, and His word is not in us"
(1John 1:8-10, HCSB).

Read I John 1:8-10, printed in the margin. How can the spiritual discipline of confession practically help you strengthen your willingness to apologize?

_____

_____

Good relationships are not dependent upon perfection but rather on a willingness to acknowledge our wrong and to seek forgiveness.

I asked Joy what she expected to hear in a genuine apology. "I want it to be sincere," she said. "I don't want him to just say 'I'm sorry that you got hurt.' I want him to acknowledge that what he did was wrong."

After explaining the emotional dynamics of Rich's family, I suggested that if she would make a specific request of Rich, it would less likely be taken as condemnation. A suggestion or a request is very different from a demand. And I encouraged her to give Rich an affirming word each time he did these things with Ethan. Here's part of the list that we came up with:

- "Would you play Chutes and Ladders with Ethan while I finish getting the meal together?"
- "Could the three of us take a walk after dinner?"
- "Would you mind giving Ethan his bath tonight?"

Obviously, Rich's primary apology language was "I'm sorry." When Joy said these words, he was ready to forgive her. Joy's primary apology language was "I was wrong." What she wanted to sense was that Rich knew that his harsh words were wrong. Their marriage took a giant step forward when she learned to express genuine regret, and he learned to accept responsibility for his wrong behavior; and they learned to verbalize it to each other.

day Five

The Power of Apology Language

Talk-show host Oprah Winfrey surprised her national television audience on January 26, 2006, by opening her program with these words: "I made a mistake." Winfrey was apologizing for defending an author who fictionalized many parts of his memoir, *A Million Little Pieces.* Her defense of James Frey on Larry King Live after Frey was found to have altered facts and misled readers alienated many of her supporters as well as book critics who found his stretching of the truth in a nonfiction work inexcusable.

Winfrey continued, "By defending Mr. Frey, I left the impression that the truth does not matter, and I am deeply sorry about that because that is not what I believe."[2] Winfrey's apology included apology language #1, *expressing regret,* as well as apology language #2, *accepting responsibility.* By accepting responsibility for her actions, Oprah restored her respect among many who were offended.

Without apologies, anger builds and pushes us to demand justice. When, as we see it, justice is not forthcoming, we often take matters into our own hands and seek revenge on those who have wronged us. When we apologize, we accept responsibility for our behavior, seeking to make amends with the person who was offended. Genuine apology opens the door to the possibility of forgiveness and reconciliation.

[1]As quoted in Gary Chapman and Jennifer Thomas's The Five Languages of Apology (Chicago: Northfield, 2006) 39.

[2]Patrick T. Reardon, "Oprah Turns on Memoir Author," Chicago Tribune, 27 January 2006, sec. 1.

❏ I know that what I did
was wrong. I could try
to excuse myself,
but there is no
excuse. Pure and
simple, what I did was
selfish and wrong.

❏ I made a big mistake.
At the time, I didn't
think much about
what I was doing. But
in retrospect, I guess
that's the problem.
I wish I had thought
before I acted. What I
did was wrong.

❏ The way I spoke to
you was wrong. It was
harsh and untrue.
I spoke out of anger,
trying to justify
myself. The way I talk-
ed to you was unkind
and unloving. I hope
you'll forgive me.

❏ I repeated a mistake
that we've discussed
before. I really
messed up. I know
that it was my fault.

Sincere apologies also assuage a guilty conscience. Picture your conscience as a five-gallon container strapped to your back. Whenever you wrong another, it's like pouring a gallon of liquid into your conscience. Three or four wrongs and you are getting heavy. A full conscience leaves one with a sense of guilt and shame. The only way to effectively empty the conscience is to apologize to God and the person you offended. When this is done, you can look God in the face, you can look yourself in the mirror, and you can look the other person in the eyes; not because you are perfect but because you have been willing to take responsibility for your failure.

Read Psalm 32. How did David's willingness to take responsibility affect his outlook?

_____

_____

Describe a time when an apology by you or someone else had a great impact.

_____

LEARNING THE LANGUAGE

Pam is twenty-seven. While growing up, her dad told her that a wise person is willing to accept responsibility for his or her mistakes. "I'll never forget what he said. 'All of us make mistakes, but the only mistake that will destroy you is the one you are unwilling to admit.'" As one lady said, "'I'm sorry' is not enough. I want to know that he understands that what he did was wrong."

For these individuals, if you want them to sense the sincerity of your apology, you might use statements such as those printed in the margin.

Read the statements of accepting responsibility printed in the margin. Check two statements that you could use in relationship situations this week.

BEFORE THE SESSION

1. Purchase or locate an inexpensive clay vase or pot. Before class, intentionally break the pottery and try to loosely piece it together with glue.
2. Pray for those in your class. Ask God to break through the stubborn resistance some might feel when it comes to admitting they were wrong and responsible.

DURING THE SESSION

1. State and then ask: *Think of a time when you broke something that was valuable to someone you love (such as a parent, sibling, friend, etc.). How did you handle the situation?* Take note of any responses where someone tried to cover up the mistake. Show the broken (and repaired) pottery piece. Say: *Sometimes we make mistakes, and like this piece of pottery, relationships are affected and even broken.* Explain that you broke this pottery and then tried to glue it back together. Ask: *Will it ever be the same?* Continue: *Are our relationships like this piece of broken and repaired pottery? Why or why not?* Explain that this series on the language of apology provides an opportunity to look at the aspects of our relationships that sometimes cause cracks. The act of an apology, well expressed and well received, empowered by the love of Jesus, actually can mend much of the brokenness in our relationships. Encourage all learners to look for opportunities to practice what they learn at work and play as well as at home with extended family.
2. Ask learners to share how they responded to the introductory questions on page 114. Direct learners to read Psalm 51. Explain that David, being a man after God's own heart, understood the art of apology. Ask learners to share words and phrases that express David's regret. Ask: *Why is it hard for us to sometimes express regret?* Encourage learners to share how Luke 18:9-14 relates to a healthy sense of regret (p. 118).
3. Ask: *In Psalm 51, how did David model regret without saying "but..."* (p. 118)? Emphasize that David's willingness to tell the honest, transparent truth was honorable to God. When we give an honest apology it is honorable to our loved ones as well. Ask: *How did you rate yourself on*

To the Leader:

Recognize that creating the right climate for class discussion is important. If your class consists of couples, create space for dialogue between couples within the class context. Regularly challenge couples to continue discussing issues at home. Emphasize on a regular basis that the impact of this study has everything to do with conversations that emerge after class time in all contexts of the learner's life.

blaming others on page 119? Ask: *Regarding Psalm 51, why do you suppose David was willing to be honest and not "pass the buck"?* Explain that sincerity is crucial in the way we apologize. Ask someone to read aloud Psalm 51:16-17 and share responses to the activity on page 119. Instruct learners to review the "Statements of Regret" listed at the end of Day 2. Ask: *Which of these statements are helpful for you as you consider people who need to hear an apology from you?*

4. Ask: *How is expressing regret different from accepting responsibility?* Call for responses to the question at the top of page 121. Ask learners to share Larry's, Jane's, and Shawn's excuses that they underlined. Ask: *Why are the responses of Larry, Jane, and Shawn lethal to good relationships?*

5. Ask learners to look at 2 Samuel 12:1-15. Explain that David was confronted by Nathan with his wrongdoing. Ask: *Which verses show that David modeled a willingness to accept responsibility? How did he respond to the wrongdoing in Nathan's story? How are his reactions in 2 Samuel similar to the way we deal with confrontation?* In answering these questions, encourage learners to share what they know about David, as well as their reflections based on how they typically react. After some discussion, ask learners to read Romans 3:23 and answer the question from page 121.

6. State: *Describe a time when it was hard to admit you were wrong.* Ask: *Why was it hard? How were you received after admitting your fault?* Explain that sometimes our unwillingness to admit fault has to do with what was modeled for us growing up. Ask learners to share how they responded to the first activity on Day 4. Ask someone to read aloud 1 John 1:8-10. Discuss the spiritual discipline of confession (see p. 124).

7. Direct learners to open their Bibles to Psalm 32. Ask for responses to both parts of the first activity in Day 5. Then ask: *Which of the "Statements of Accepting Responsibility" resonate with you the most?*

8. Hold up the repaired pottery piece. Ask: *Based on what we know from God's Word, are we able to mend the breaks in our relationships?* Adamantly emphasize that we can and that God wants us to be about the work of reconciliation—starting with our marriages and families. Challenge learners to identify one way they can exercise both the languages of expressing regret and accepting responsibility in the days to come.

Making Restitution

Making Things Right

The idea of "making things right" to make up for a wrong is embedded within the human psyche. Something deep within us says, "If I have been wronged, someone needs to pay." Parents seek to teach children this principle. When a mother sees a four-year-old son grab a doll from the hands of his six-year-old sister, the mother requires him not only to say "I'm sorry" but to also return the doll.

This reality surfaced again and again in our research. Over and over again people made statements such as the following:

- "I expect some sense of contrition but also a sincere effort to amend the damage caused by the rift."
- "I expect him to try to repair what has gone wrong."
- "I expect her to be truly sorry from the heart and be willing to make things right."
- "I want him to make amends as appropriate. Things don't just go away by saying 'I'm sorry.'"

All of these individuals viewed the effort to "make things right" as the strongest evidence of the sincerity of the apology. Their primary apology language is *making restitution*.

Read Luke 19:1-10. How did Zacchaeus attempt to make restitution? What was Jesus' reaction?

_____

_____

_____

"I OUGHT TO DO SOMETHING TO MAKE AMENDS"

The New Webster's Dictionary defines *restitution* as "the act of giving back to a rightful owner" or "a giving of something as an equivalent for what has been lost, damaged, etc." In his book *Since Nobody's Perfect . . . How Good Is Good Enough?* Andy Stanley writes, "A willingness to do something to try to make up for the pain I have caused you is evidence of a true apology. A voice inside us says, 'I ought to do something to make amends for what I have done.'"[1]

Everett Worthington Jr., professor of psychology at Virginia Commonwealth University and a leader in research on forgiveness, calls the act of making such amends "equalizing." He says:

> Equalizing is making up for the loss that the other person experienced. To offer restitution is to equalize the balance of justice. Any hurt or offense causes the person who is hurt to lose something. Perhaps he or she loses self-esteem, self-respect, or a tangible benefit (such as if I offend you in front of your boss and you lose a promotion opportunity). So it is an act of kindness for the transgressor to offer to make up for the loss.[2]

If restitution is the primary apology language of an individual, then this becomes the most important part of the apology. "I'm sorry; I was wrong" will never be taken as sincere if these words are not accompanied by a sincere effort at restitution. Without your effort to make amends, the apology will not have the desired results of forgiveness and reconciliation.

"Without your effort to make amends, the apology will not have the desired results of forgiveness and reconciliation."

—Gary Chapman

Regarding your life, in what specific situation would restitution, of some sort, help in the reconciliation process? How can you practically institute the process of restitution in this situation?

_____

_____

_____

The Need for Love

"DO YOU STILL LOVE ME?"

In the private sphere of family and other close relationships, our desire for restitution is almost always based upon our need for love. After being hurt deeply, we need the reassurance that the person who hurt us still loves us. After all, successful family relationships and true friendships ultimately are based on love.

When we are hurt by the words or behavior of a family member, we often feel angry. The reason it hurts so deeply and the anger is so intense is that we desperately want to be loved by that person. Harsh words or hurtful actions have called into question that love.

> **What specific harsh words and actions, directed toward you, have left a wound that refuses to heal in your life?**

_____

_____

"How could they love me and do that?" is the question that lingers in our minds. The words "I'm sorry; I was wrong" may not be enough. We want to know the answer to the question, "Do you still love me?" It is the answer to this question that requires restitution.

For people whose primary apology language is making restitution, the statement, "It is not right for me to have treated you that way," must be followed with "What can I do to show you that I still care about you?" Without this effort at restitution, this person will question the sincerity of the apology. He or she will continue to feel unloved even though you may have said, "I am sorry; I was wrong." The person waits for the tangible reassurance that you genuinely love him or her.

Read 1 Corinthians 13:4-8. How could this description of love apply to the process of restitution? Write your thoughts in the margin.

WHEN THE MESSAGE ISN'T GETTING THROUGH

The question, then, is how do we make restitution in the most effective way? Some husbands have the idea that the best way to express restitution is by flowers. However, the gift of flowers is not the love language of all women. That's why some husbands have had their flowers pushed back into their faces, while the wives walk away in disgust, saying, "He thinks flowers solve everything!"

In the chart below, list in the left column ways you try to show love. In the right column, express how well your expression is usually received. Show your responses to your spouse (family member, friend, colleague). Ask him or her to react and give feedback.

Ways you try to show love	How this expression of love is received

In making restitution, one size does not fit all. That is why many husbands and wives have been frustrated in their efforts to "make it right." It seemed that no matter what they did, they could not do enough. The problem is that they were not speaking their spouse's primary love language. Therefore, the message of restitution—reaffirming love—was not getting through. Since the heart of restitution is reassuring the spouse or family member that you genuinely love him or her, it is essential to express restitution in the love language of the other person. And during the next two days I will show you how you can do just that.

The Language of Restitution

Effective restitution requires learning the love language of the person you love and speaking it as a part of your apology.

LEARNING THE FIVE LOVE LANGUAGES

After thirty-five years of marriage and family counseling, I am convinced that there are fundamentally five emotional *love languages*. Each person has one of the five as a primary language. If you speak his/her primary love language, he/she will be reassured of your love, and restitution will be successful. However, if you don't speak the primary love language, your best efforts at apologizing may not be successful. Therefore, let me review briefly the five love languages and illustrate how speaking the primary love language will make your efforts at restitution successful.

For an in-depth look at expressing the five love languages among adults, see *The Five Love Languages* (Chicago: Northfield, 1992) and *The Five Love Languages for Singles* (Chicago: Northfield, 2003). Available at *www.lifeway.com*.

Words of Affirmation

Love language number one is *words of affirmation*. Using words to affirm the other person may focus on his/her personality, behavior, dress, accomplishments, or beauty. The important thing is that words communicate verbally your affection and appreciation for the person.

Here are a couple of examples from our research of people for whom words of affirmation is their primary love language and how hearing those words made their spouse's efforts at restitution successful.

Megan is twenty-nine and has been married to Brad for six years. "I know that Brad's apology is sincere when he retracts his hurtful words and then tells me how much he loves me. Sometimes he goes to the extreme in telling me how wonderful I am and how sorry he is that he hurt me. I guess he knows that it takes a lot of positive words to make up for the hurtful things he has said."

Tim said, "It's those words 'You are so wonderful' that get me. I've never failed to forgive her because I know she's sincere. We all make mistakes; I don't expect her to be perfect. But it surely feels good when she tells me how wonderful I am while asking me to forgive her."

For Tim and Megan, words of affirmation are all the restitution they need. That's their favorite part of an apology.

Mark on the top of this scale of 1 to 10 how important "affirmation" is in the way your spouse (family member or friend) relates to you. Underneath, mark how important you think affirmation is to that person.

├─────┼─────┼─────┼─────┼─────┼─────┼─────┼─────┼─────┤

Acts of Service

The second love language, *acts of service*, is based on the old axiom "Actions speak louder than words." For these people, love is demonstrated by thoughtful acts of kindness.

Gwen was visibly upset. "I'm sick and tired of his apologies," she said. "'I'm sorry, I'm sorry, I'm sorry.' That's all he ever says. What I want to know is: Does he still love me, or does he want out of the marriage? If he loves me, then why doesn't he do something to help me around the house? I'm tired of living with a man who sits in front of the TV while I cook the meals and wash the dishes. I work outside the home as well as he. How can he love me and do nothing? Actions speak louder than words."

After explaining the five love languages to Gwen, the couple made the effort to discover each other's primary love language. Her husband, Mark, realized that a verbal apology to her was never enough. It had to involve restitution—the reassurance of his love—and this needed to be expressed in acts of service. I don't see Mark often, but when I do, he always thanks me for the insights on love and apology that "saved my marriage."

This same principle applies in friendships. One day, as a practical joke, Steve commandeered Ben's office computer while Ben was away. Steve pretended to be Ben and sent out an e-mail to their six-person work group, inviting them all to come to Ben's house for a New Year's Eve dinner party. When he was alerted to the counterfeit invitation by a colleague, Ben felt angry and betrayed.

When confronted by Ben, Steve offered a sincere apology. Before Ben could accept the apology, however, he needed Steve to make things right.

At Ben's insistence, Steve sent out a correction e-mail to the work group. This retraction allowed Ben to feel that Steve had owned up to the problem he had created and set things right again.

On a scale of 1 to 10 how important are "acts of service" in the way your spouse (family member or friend) relates to you?

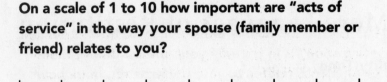

How important are acts of service to that person?

Receiving Gifts

For some people, *receiving gifts* is their primary love language. Therefore, if the person you've offended prefers the love language of receiving gifts and you wish to make amends for the wrong you have done, giving gifts will be an effective method of restitution.

Bethany finds her husband's apologies sincere, because he speaks her language. "He makes his apology; then that evening, he brings me a rose to make up for what he has done that has offended me. I don't know what it is, but the rose seems to communicate to me that he really is sincere. So I forgive him."

With their son sick with leukemia and often in the hospital, Susan tried to understand her husband's tenseness. "A lot of pain and anger was taken out on me, but I let it slide off because I understood. Out of the blue one day, he walked into the hospital room with flowers and a card and a full apology for taking his stress out on me. It was one of the most tender times in our marriage. He realized by his own conviction that he was hurting me, and he took the initiative to apologize. The flowers and the card sealed it for me. I knew he was sincere." He not only apologized, but he made restitution by speaking Susan's love language, receiving gifts.

On a scale of 1 to 10 how important is "receiving gifts" in the way your spouse (family member, friend) relates to you?

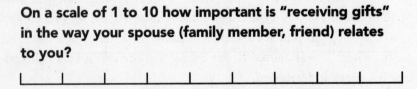

How important is receiving gifts to that person?

More Language of Restitution

Quality Time

Love language number four is *quality time*. Giving another person your undivided attention communicates, "You are important to me." Quality time means no distractions. The TV is off; the magazine is on the table along with the book. You are not paying the bills; you are not looking at a computer screen. Such times do not even need to include major activities or projects together; they can simply be extended conversations between two individuals. For those individuals, giving your undivided attention while making the apology is restitution enough. It communicates deeply to the person that he or she is loved.

Mary from St. Louis recalls a powerful apology she received. As she sat with her husband at lunch after a marriage conference, Phil took her hands and thanked her for buying the tickets to the conference.

She says, "He told me that it had opened his eyes and challenged him to be the husband he had neglected to be for the past five years of our marriage. The fact that he set aside time to talk to me and to apologize for his actions the past week was almost more than I could believe. In the past every time he tried to apologize, he would say 'I'm sorry,' and that was it. But this time, I knew that he was sincere, and I freely forgave him."

Phil was speaking Mary's love language, quality time, and that made all the difference.

On a scale of 1 to 10 how important is "quality time" in the way your spouse (family member, friend) relates to you?

How important is quality time to that person?

Physical Touch

Love language number five is *physical touch*. Holding hands, kissing, embracing, putting an arm around the shoulder, giving a pat on the back, or running your hand through someone's hair are all expressions of the language of physical touch. We're not talking just husbands and wives. Physical touch is appropriate among all family members, including mothers and sons and fathers and daughters.

When Judson, married for fifteen years, says, "After granting forgiveness, there has to be a hug for the apology process to be complete," he is clearly revealing that he expects restitution to be a part of the apology process, and physical touch is the language of love which he understands best. After the hug, he feels that his wife has "made amends" for her wrong. Without the hug, the apology process is lacking something important for him.

Robert knew that his words had been extremely hurtful to Jake, his ten-year-old son. After expressing his apology, he walked over to Jake, put his arms around him, and gave him a big bear hug. When he gained his composure, his father looked him in the eyes and said, "I love you so much." And Jake said, "I love you too, Dad," as he gave his father a hug around the neck. His father's apology was effective because he made restitution by speaking his son's primary love language, physical touch.

If physical touch is one's primary love language and I want to make a sincere apology, then I must communicate restitution by reaching out to give affirming touches. Words alone will not suffice. It is the touch that makes amends for the wrongs.

On a scale of 1 to 10 how important is "physical touch" in the way your spouse (family member or friend) relates to you?

L———l———l———l———l———l———l———l———l———l

How important is physical touch to that person?

Suggestion:

After working through the activities for Days 3 and 4, share your responses with your spouse (family member or friend). Allow the person to react and give feedback in order to see if you clearly understand his or her "love language needs."

day *Five*

Repaying and Restoring

At age seventeen, Paula stole her grandparents' car while they were away on vacation, took a joyride, wrecked the car, and ended up in the hospital. Two days later when her grandparents returned, they visited Paula. She knew she had failed two important people who loved her very much. So she apologized profusely.

Her grandfather said very slowly, "Paula, what you did has disappointed us greatly. We know you are sorry right now, and we know that you regret what you did. But if you really want to sincerely apologize, then you will have to repay whatever it costs to get the car repaired. Then we'll know that your apology is sincere. We love you. We want the best for you, but we cannot overlook what you have done. So whenever you get well, we'll work out a payment schedule."

When they left the room, Paula was in a state of shock. She never dreamed her grandfather would respond that way. She thought he would freely forgive her if she apologized and cried. She did not understand two things. First, her grandfather's apology language was making restitution. To him an apology was not sincere if it did not include making restitution for the wrong that was done. Second, her grandfather knew that if she suffered no consequences for her actions, it would simply be a matter of time until she would do something just as harmful and perhaps worse.

Restitution often extends beyond expressing love through speaking one of the five languages of love. It may require repayment or restoring of something taken—a damaged car, a scratched watch, or even a good name. The desire to make amends for one's wrong behavior is a natural part of apologizing if one is indeed sincere.

Describe a time when you had to make restitution for a wrong.

[1] Andy Stanley, *Since Nobody's Perfect...How Good Is Good Enough?* (Sisters, OR.: Multnomah Publishers, Inc., 2003), 72.

[2] Everett L. Worthington Jr., *Forgiving and Reconciling* (Downers Grove: InterVarsity Press, 2003), 205.

Did your situation look like Paula's? How was your situation similar? How was it different?

_____

_____

A TAX COLLECTOR MAKES AMENDS

The story of Zacchaeus that you read earlier in the week is a fascinating story recorded in the life of Jesus. You might want to reread Luke 19:1-10.

Zacchaeus was shocked and deeply moved that Jesus would actually visit in his home. Apparently Zacchaeus recognized that he was dealing with a man who knew of his self-centered lifestyle and yet was willing to associate with him. Immediately, Zacchaeus apologized for his wrong behavior through the years and then said that he planned to repay all those from whom he had taken funds unjustly. In fact, he promised to repay them four times as much as he had taken. Jesus interpreted this as the sign of a genuine confession, and He even held up Zacchaeus as an example of how to deal with failure.

A genuine apology will be accompanied by a desire to right the wrongs committed, to make amends for the damage done, and to assure the person that you genuinely care about him or her.

Describe an experience in your life that reflects the spirit of confession modeled by Zacchaeus.

_____

_____

If you are not certain what the offended person might consider proper restitution, you might ask questions like the ones listed in the margin.

Think again about someone with whom you need to make amends. Look at the statements of restitution in the margin. Identify statements that reflect how you can initiate the process of restitution. Seek to use one or more of these statements in the days to come as you seek to restore your relationship with someone.

STATEMENTS OF RESTITUTION

❑ Is there anything I can do to make up for what I have done?

❑ I know I have hurt you deeply, and I feel like I should do something to repay you for the hurt I've caused. Can you give me a suggestion?

❑ I know that I've inconvenienced you. May I give you some of my time to balance things out?

❑ I regret that I've damaged your honor. May I make a (public) correction?

❑ I've broken this promise a million times. Would you like for me to put my commitment to you in writing this time?

139

Before the Session

1. Bring in examples of items that symbolize ways we make restitution to others (i.e., money, a card, flowers, etc.). Set up a table and place these items on display so that learners will notice them when coming into class.
2. Make available a whiteboard and dry erase marker.
3. Pray for learners in your class who may be overwhelmed with the idea of restitution because of the depth of what they have done to hurt someone in the past.

During the Session

1. Say: "It is one thing to *say* you are sorry. It is another to *show* that you are sorry." Explain that the lessons this week provide practical and thoughtful tips as to how you show your apology through making things right. Call attention to the third apology language at the beginning of Day 1. Ask learners to define the word *restitution*. Refer to the definitions offered on page 130. Ask: *How do we typically make restitution?* Point to the items displayed. Explain that these are examples of ways people sometimes try to make things right. Ask: *What other things do you do to try to "make it right" with someone?* Ask someone to read aloud Luke 19:1-10. Ask: *How did Zacchaeus attempt to make restitution? What was Jesus' reaction?* [See the first activity in Day 1.] Ask if anyone would like to share how he or she responded to the activity on page 130.

2. In Day 2, Chapman and Thomas say that "successful family relationships and true friendships are ultimately based on love." Ask: *Was this your experience growing up? Why or why not? What contributed to a sense of love in your home growing up? What contributes to a sense of love in your home now?* Explain that love gives us a sense of safety. In the same way, an absence of love can leave us feeling wounded in significant ways. Invite learners to share how they responded to the first activity on Day 2.

3. Ask someone to read aloud 1 Corinthians 13:4-8. Ask learners to share how they applied this Scripture to the process of restitution. Explain that 1 Corinthians 13:4-8 reflects the active nature of love. We show our feelings of love through many expressions. Ask learners to share any insights they came up with after filling out the chart on page 132.

4. Five love languages are addressed in Days 3 and 4. Ask someone to list them on a whiteboard. Explain that more information concerning these love languages is available in the book *The Five Love Languages* by Gary Chapman. Ask learners to share how they responded to the activity scales that followed each love language description (see activities for both Day 3 and 4). Ask: *What seems to be your primary love language? Were you surprised by anything you discovered as you learned about each language?*

5. Ask: *Which of the love languages best reflects what you see in your spouse or loved one?* Call attention to the suggestion for couples in the margin of Day 4. Ask couples who feel comfortable in doing so to share any results from their discussions. Ask: *Did you and your spouse agree or disagree with how you each perceived each other's top love language? How would your individual love languages affect the way you each offered or would want to receive an apology?* Explain that nothing is better that talking with each other to clarify what each other values when it comes to love language preferences. Remind learners to also seek friends, co-workers, or family members with whom they need to apply what they are learning about apology language. Ask if anyone has a workplace or other situation they would like to talk about. Allow time for discussion.

6. As a class, reread Paula's story from Day 5. After reading, allow learners to share how they responded to the first activity for Day 5. After discussing Paula's situation, reread Luke 19:1-10 aloud. Ask: *How is Zacchaeus's story an example of "repaying"? How is it a story of restoration? Who experienced the most restoration? Why?*

7. Conclude this lesson by allowing learners to spend time reflecting on their responses to the last activity on Day 5. Review the "Statements of Restitution" listed in the margin. Look in particular at the first statement of restitution—"Is there anything I can do to make up for what I have done?" Ask: *Would you be willing to ask this question of someone you have deeply wronged? Why or why not? Why is it scary to make yourself open and vulnerable to "do what you have to do" in order to make up?*

8. Ask learners to look again at the table with the items of restitution that are on display. Ask: *What do you need to do this week to specifically and tangibly bring restitution into a broken relationship?* Conclude by praying together as a class.

Genuinely Repenting

day One

Repentance Is the Heart

Genuinely Repenting

"I'll try not to do that again."

Repentance is more than saying, "I'm sorry; I was wrong. How can I make this up to you?" It is saying, "I'll try not to do this again." What people who have been hurt want to know is, "Do you intend to change, or will this happen again next week?" The offending person's repentance, then, elicits the offended person's forgiveness.

In our research, we asked the question, "What do you expect in an apology?" Repeatedly we heard statements like the following:

- "Show that you are willing to change, and do it differently next time."
- "I expect them to find ways to stop it from happening again."
- "I want them to have a plan for improvement, a plan to succeed and not to fail."

These and scores of similar statements reveal that for many people, repentance is at the heart of a true apology. The language of *genuinely repenting* convinces them that the apology is sincere.

How do you define the word *repentance*?

_____

Read Matthew 4:17. Why do you suppose Jesus urgently prioritized the message found in this one verse? How do you suppose the content of this message is helpful as we think about our relationships?

_____

_____

"I WANT TO CHANGE"

How then do we speak the language of repentance? We recognize that what we have done is wrong, that our actions have hurt the one we love. We don't want to continue this behavior; therefore, we decide that with God's help, we will change. Then we verbalize this decision to the person we have offended. It is the decision to change that indicates that we are no longer making excuses. We are not minimizing our behavior but are accepting full responsibility for our actions.

When we share our intention to change with the person we have offended, he or she gets a glimpse of our heart—and this often is the language that convinces the person we mean what we say.

Jim, thirty-five, explained what he seeks in an apology. "I expect the persons to come to me and sit down face-to-face, not over the phone, and tell me that they were wrong and tell me that they're going to make changes so that it won't happen again. I want them to be realistic and tell me that they know they have to work on it so I should be patient with them." Whether it's a coworker or family member, Jim is willing to wait for those changes. "I know that changes don't happen overnight, but admitting that you are willing to work on changing is what's important to me."

Some may resist the idea of verbally expressing an intention to change for fear they will not actually change. Your philosophy may be, "Just make the changes; don't talk about them." The problem with that approach is that the offended person cannot read your mind. When you state your intention to change, the person knows that you truly recognize that your behavior is wrong—and that you fully intend to change the behavior.

It is perfectly fine to tell them that you hope they will be patient with you because you know you will not be 100 percent successful immediately but that it is your intention to change this destructive behavior. Now they know your intention and sense that your apology is sincere so they can now forgive you even before the changes are actually made.

> "When you state your intention to change, the person knows that you truly recognize that your behavior is wrong—and that you fully intend to change the behavior."
>
> —Gary Chapman

"I'LL APOLOGIZE, BUT I WON'T CHANGE"

Craig is by nature a joker—jovial, always making a humorous comment. The problem is that many of his jokes are off-color. This greatly offends and embarrasses his wife, Betty. Craig is willing to say, "I'm sorry I offended you. It is not my intention to hurt you." But he is not willing to say, "I was wrong, and I will change the kind of jokes I tell."

In my office, he defended himself by saying, "No one else finds my jokes offensive." With a little research, we found out that statement was untrue. A number of people, especially women in his office, found his jokes offensive. They had simply not taken the initiative to confront him.

A few weeks later when I shared this information with Craig, he began to think differently. However, it should not have taken this information for Craig to have repented of his behavior. The fact that it deeply hurt his wife and created a huge emotional barrier between the two of them should have been enough to motivate him to make changes. When Craig realized it was change or lose his marriage, he was willing to change. That was fourteen years ago. Today Craig and Betty have a strong marriage. They even lead a marriage enrichment class in their church.

The idea that we only need to make changes when we are doing something morally wrong is erroneous.

Read Romans 14:13 and 19, printed in the margin. Paul encouraged believers to seek what would

_____ _____ **and** _____ _____.

In the margin indicate how you can apply this admonition to a behavior pattern in your life that is hard to change. How has this behavior affected relationships in your life?

"Therefore, let us no longer criticize one another, but instead decide not to put a stumbling block or pitfall in your brother's way" (Rom. 14:13, HCSB).

"So then, we must pursue what promotes peace and what builds up one another" (Rom. 14:19, HCSB).

day *Two*

Beyond Words—To Real Change

The second step down the road of repentance is developing a plan for implementing change. Often apologies fail to be successful in restoring the relationship because there is no plan for making positive changes. One wife said, "Flowers and apologies were typical after his womanizing episodes. The problem is there were never any changes. I eventually got sick of his apologies and threw his flowers in his face. We've been divorced ten years now."

"HE'S A GOOD MAN. I DON'T WANT TO LOSE HIM."

I met Rick and Rita in New Orleans. He explained that after reading *The Five Love Languages* a year earlier, he realized his love languages are physical touch and quality time. He told this to Rita and thought her speaking his love languages would help their marriage.

"At the time, I was feeling really unloved by her," Rick said, with Rita standing at his side. "She spent all of her time with her mother and her friends. I felt like she was married to them more than she was married to me. At the time she told me she was sorry, that she did not want to hurt me, that she loved me very much, and that she would try to speak my love languages, but that was the end of it. Nothing ever changed. It was like we didn't even have the conversation.

"Would you sincerely like to have a better marriage?" I asked Rita.

"I really would," she said. "He's a good man, and I don't want to lose him." In the next five minutes I mapped out a plan for her on how to learn to speak the love language of physical touch. Then I shared some ideas about quality time. I challenged her to sit down with Rick for fifteen minutes on Monday, Wednesday, and Friday nights and discuss their day and how things went. I told her she would find other ideas on how to speak the language of quality time in the book and urged her to read that chapter again.

Six months later I received a letter. Rick said, "Dr. Chapman, Rita took your plan seriously. She has become extremely fluent in speaking my love languages." Rita made changes once she had a plan. She had the desire to meet Rick's needs much earlier, but the desire was not turned into reality until she adopted a plan for making changes. Plans need not be elaborate, but they need to be specific.

> "Plans need not be elaborate, but they need to be specific."
> —Gary Chapman

MAKE A SPECIFIC PLAN

Sometimes the offended party will be able to help you work out a plan. One night Chet strongly rebuked his four-year-old son out of his own anger and frustration. Clara had recently studied the apology languages. She explained to Chet that she needed an apology and that she also wanted a plan so that it would never happen again. Clara said, "I needed to know he was committed to making that plan work.

"Before I knew about the apology languages, I would have accepted his initial weak apology. I would have walked away feeling hurt and angry.

A bit of intimacy would have been eaten away from our marriage. Instead, just the opposite happened. I identified what I needed and he provided it. He fully repented and admitted he was wrong."

The two worked together on a plan. Clara told me that a part of the plan they worked out together was that if her husband felt himself getting angry with the children, he would go to her and say, "I'm getting heated. Will you please take over?" He would take a walk around the block and come back and try to help her in any way he could. "So far the plan is working really well," Clara said.

It is ideal when couples can help each other work out a plan to correct a behavior that is troublesome to one of them.

Think about behavior patterns you know you need to change. Plan a time to sit with your spouse (family member or friend) and make a specific plan as to how you can change your patterns. Jot down ideas in the margin.

day *Three*

Making It Work

The third step down the road of repentance is implementing the plan. A plan that is not implemented is like a seed that is not planted. Making the plan work requires thought and action.

Read James 1:22-25. How do these verses relate to the way we practically live out repentance?

_____

_____

_____

PUT IT IN WRITING!

I have often found it helpful to write on an index card the changes I am trying to implement and to post them on the mirror where I shave in the mornings. It is a way of keeping them on the front burner of my mind. I am more likely to make the changes if I am consciously aware of what I am trying to do differently today.

Writing it down also helps make the plan concrete and specific rather than general. For example, a general plan might be, "I will try not to blame her for my negative emotions." A more specific plan might be, "I will start my sentences with 'I' rather than 'you.'" Example: "I feel angry," rather than "You make me angry." This is a plan that you are more likely to implement, because it is specific.

SMALL CHANGES, BIG DIFFERENCE

Joel's wife, Joyce, was quarrelsome. It seemed to Joel that almost everything she said was negative, and whatever he said, she disagreed with. In our counseling sessions it became obvious to me that for Joyce the world was either black or white. She tended to see everything as good or bad, right or wrong. Thus, if she disagreed with Joel's idea, his idea was "wrong."

One of the plans Joyce developed was that if she disagreed with Joel's idea, she would first give an affirming statement and then share her opinion. We actually wrote out three affirming statements that she might try.

1. "That's an interesting way to look at it."
2. "I can appreciate that."
3. "One of the things I like about that idea is...."

When sharing her opinions, Joyce agreed that she would start her sentences with, "My perception of that is." Joel indicated that he thought that this plan would make a great deal of difference for him and that he would really appreciate Joyce's efforts to respect his opinions.

COUNTING THE COST

Sometimes implementing the plan for change can be extremely costly. Caroline came to me for counseling to help her deal with depression and feelings of betrayal. She had married an attractive, professional athlete named Chris when they were each twenty-two years old. Shortly after the birth of their first child, Chris had begun an affair with a younger woman. When confronted by Caroline about the affair, he admitted wrongdoing and said that he wanted to repair the marriage. For Caroline, it was critical for her to hear from Chris that he was not only sorry for his wrong action but that he would make changes in his lifestyle.

In the end, Chris made a very drastic change. He left the professional sports world and took a desk job in order to avoid temptation. In addition, Chris worked to rebuild Caroline's trust by telling her where he would be and opening up his cell phone and e-mail accounts to his wife.

Caroline needed to know that things would be different in the future, and Chris offered these concessions in order to reestablish trust. Caroline forgave Chris, and five years later, they have a strong marriage.

"At first, I couldn't believe that Chris would make all of those changes for me. I didn't even ask him to give up his athletic career, but his actions spoke volumes to me. I have never doubted his sincerity or his commitment. I feel so loved by him," she said.

The plan may call for huge changes or minor changes; it may involve huge issues or minor details.

Grab some index cards and apply Dr. Chapman's suggestion for making a plan. List changes you can initiate that will help make a difference. Share your ideas with your spouse (family member or friend). Ask for feedback.

day *Four*

What If We Fail?

"One or two setbacks does not mean that you are a failure in following your plan for change."

—Gary Chapman

Just because we're working on a plan for constructive change does not mean we will immediately be successful. There are often failures along the road even when we are sincerely trying. These failures need not defeat us. One or two setbacks does not mean that you are a failure in following your plan for change. The key is being willing to admit your failures and get up and try again.

ACKNOWLEDGE YOUR FAILURE QUICKLY

It's better when you can acknowledge any subsequent failure quickly, even before the offended person has time to confront you. When we fail to admit our relapses, it communicates to the spouse that we were not sincere in our apology. I met Judy at a marriage seminar in Seattle. She shared this story: "My husband, Steve, criticized me for being afraid of heights. He knew this about me before we got married, but it didn't seem to bother him then. I confronted him about it and told him how much it hurt and embarrassed me. I told him that I was willing to talk to a counselor but, in the meantime, I would appreciate it if he wouldn't mention it. He apologized and agreed that he would never say anything about it again."

Two months later, they were on vacation at the Grand Canyon. Steve got out on an overlook, very close to the edge, and asked Judy to join him. When she refused, he said, "Look, we flew in an airplane to get out here. Now we are just standing on a rock. It won't hurt you. Come on."

Before Judy could respond, Steve realized what he had said and corrected himself. "I did it again! I can't believe I said that."

His acknowledgment and apology before Judy could even react impressed her as the real thing. "It was so sincere that I truly forgave him."

What is your reaction when you do something you vowed to stop? how about when someone you love does something he or she vowed to stop? How do you typically react?

_____

_____

Read the verses printed in the margin. Record what your reaction could be with God's help.

GET UP AND TRY AGAIN

Admitting wrong and confessing that wrong to God and to another trusted person does require both humility and honesty, but it also gives the opportunity to begin anew. When in an effort to change you "fall off the wagon," get up and try again. The tragedy is that people often give

"Do nothing out of rivalry or conceit, but in humility consider others as more important than yourselves. Everyone should look out not only for his own interests, but also for the interests of others" (Phil. 2:3-4, HCSB).

"And be kind and compassionate to one another, forgiving one another, just as God also forgave you in Christ" (Eph. 4:32, HCSB).

up when they are next door to success. Old behavior patterns die slowly, but we will be successful if we continue to work out our changes.

Bob Tries—and Tries Again

Bob and I worked out a plan for changing his critical comments and increasing his words of affirmation to his wife Anne. It seemed that many of his critical comments had come within the first fifteen minutes after he arrived home in the evening. He would see things that hadn't been done and make a comment, or he would express frustration with the behavior of the children. Anne was busy trying to get dinner ready and found these comments quite painful. She proposed the idea of Bob holding his comments on the things he found frustrating until later in the evening when they could sit down and talk about them. Bob came up with the idea to focus on giving her positive words when he first came home and to try to help with the children while she finished dinner.

Two weeks later Bob said to me, "I didn't realize this was going to be so hard. I guess I was more set in my ways than I realized. The first evening, we had a very good evening. However, the second evening I walked in and said, 'Why is Tony playing in the yard by himself? He's only two. He shouldn't be out there alone, and besides that, the neighbor's dog was licking his face.' Anne responded, 'I didn't know he was outside.'

"Then I said, 'What do you mean you didn't know he was outside? What have you been doing?' Before I knew what happened, we were into a royal argument and had a miserable evening.

"At work I began to think. I wouldn't give up on my customer. I would continue to cultivate friendship and seek to make a sale, so why would I give up on seeking to improve things in my marriage? That night I went home and told Anne how much I loved her and that I was sorry that for the last two days I had been silent. I told her that I had been processing things, that I really wanted her to know how much I loved her, and that I was not giving up on changing my behavior.

"After that, I began to stop on my way home about a block from my house and ask myself, 'What positive comment will I make to her when I get home?' It may sound a little contrived, but it helped me focus on what I needed to do."

Most people do not expect perfection after an apology, but they do expect to see effort. When the spouse gives up quickly after a failure and reverts to old behavior with no further effort to change, the apology is considered insincere. The person who apologizes may be sincere at the moment, but failure to follow through with repentance renders the apology empty.

Read Galatians 6:1-5. How can we specifically use Paul's advice from Galatians to help each other tackle sin habits within our relationships? Make your notes in the margin.

The Road Toward Change

Owen was being honest with me when he said, "I don't want to promise that I'll change, because I might fail." Changing long-standing patterns of behavior can be difficult but first you must decide that they need to be changed and, with the help of God, you will start walking down the road toward positive change. Don't allow the fear of failure to keep you from taking the initial steps down the road of repentance and success.

I am not suggesting that you promise that you will never do it again. But expressing the intention to try to change is the first step in speaking the apology language of repentance. What you are expressing is that you are going to make every effort not to repeat this behavior. It is effort that leads to success. If this is the other person's primary apology language, nothing will take the place of the words "I'm really going to try had to change this behavior." Then developing a plan and following it leads you further down the road to success and the healing of past hurts.

Inviting the offended person to help you come up with a plan for change is perhaps the best way to effectively show repentance. Here is one way to include that person: *This is such a long-term pattern for me. While I want to change, I know it will be hard, and I may fail, hurting you again along the way. I would really appreciate it if you would help me think about*

STATEMENTS OF GENUINE REPENTANCE

❑ I know that my behavior was very painful to you. I don't ever want to do that again. I'm open to any ideas you have on how I might change my behavior.

❑ I know that what I am doing is not helpful. What would you like to see me change that would make this better for you?

❑ I really do want to change. I know I'm not going to be perfect, but I really want to try to change this behavior. Would you be willing to remind me if I revert to my old patterns? Just say "relapse." I think that will help me to stop and change my direction.

❑ I let you down by making the same mistake again. What will it take for you to begin to rebuild your trust in me?

a way to help my changes stick and encourage me when you see me doing things that help. Can I count on you to be my teammate in this?

Read 1 Corinthians 13:4-8 and Romans 12:9-13. How do these verses create the right climate for encouraging change in oneself and in others?

_____

_____

_____

Review the statements of genuine repentance. Which of these four suggestions would be helpful as you work on the art of repentance in your life? Plan to use one or more of these statements as you relate to your spouse (family member or friend) in the coming days. Use the space below to write out what you plan to say.

Before the Session

1. Draw a directional arrow (➜) on index cards, one per participant. Before the session, place these arrows on the floor around the classroom making a path for learners to follow before taking their seats. Write the word *SIN* on one sheet of paper with a marker. Hold this sheet.

2. Bring extra index cards to class.

3. Pray that learners grasp the importance of repentance as it is connected to apologies, and, more importantly, as connected to our spiritual authenticity. In this lesson, we dig at the heart. We ask people to think about how an apology is connected to spiritual life-change. Without repentance, our apology is only a brief interval between repeating our mistake again!

During the Session

1. As learners enter, explain that they need to follow the path of arrows that has been laid out. After everyone has arrived, ask: *How did it feel to follow the arrows? Why did you follow the arrows?* Explain that arrow signs are a daily part of our lives. Ask: *How many arrow signs did you see before getting to class today?*

2. Ask the learners to take one of the arrow sheets from the ground and then return to their seats. Place the sheet with the word *SIN* where everyone can see it. Ask the learners to point their arrows toward the sign. Explain that Chapman and Thomas define *repentance* as "changing one's mind." Explain that while we have the habit of directing ourselves toward sin, repentance is making a change in the direction away from sin. Ask learners to turn their arrows away from the word *SIN*. Explain that they have illustrated a definition of *repentance*—"to turn away from."

3. Read aloud Matthew 4:17. Discuss the activity with this verse on page 142. Read this statement taken from Dr. Chapman's research: "A sincere apology should have a component of willingness not to repeat the offense." Ask: *How do you think an apology is affected if we refuse to change the patterns of our life?* Ask someone to read the quotation in the margin of page 145. Ask learners to reflect on how they carried out the last activity of Day 2.

4. Ask someone to read aloud James 1:22-25. Explain that repentance is not a passive endeavor. Instead, it requires intentional effort. Ask: *How does James 1:22-25 relate to the way we practically live out repentance?* (p. 146). Discuss practical ways that Dr. Chapman suggested for implementing a specific plan. Ask learners who are comfortable doing so to share information from the last activity on Day 3. If learners have yet to carry out this challenge, encourage them to use index cards to fill out specific plans for a repentant change.

5. Ask: *What is your typical reaction when you do something you vowed to stop?* Allow learners to share how they responded to this question in the first activity of Day 4 (p. 149). Follow-up by asking: *How about when someone you love does something he or she vowed to stop? How do you typically react?* Explain that no one ever said that repentance was going to be easy! It is hard and sometimes frustrating. Yet we must remember the grace of God found in Jesus. We can get up and try again because Jesus loves us and is patient with us! Ask someone to read aloud Galatians 6:1-5. Encourage learners to share how these verses apply. Emphasize that we need each other in order to tackle the challenge of repentance. God designed us to help one another. Ask: *Who helps you tackle your repentance-challenges? If you can't name anyone, why do you think that is so?*

6. Ask volunteers to read aloud 1 Corinthians 13:4-8 and Romans 12:9-13. Ask: *How do these verses create the right climate for encouraging change in one's self and in others?* Emphasize that love is the key to creating space for spiritual change and transformation.

7. Direct the learners to take the arrow cards used earlier. Ask learners to write on the blank side an attitude(s) or action(s) that is harming their relationships. After people have had time to write down their thoughts, point to the sheet of paper on the floor with the word SIN. Say: *Look at your arrow. Are you heading toward whatever it is you've placed on your card. Or are you heading, in repentance mode, away from whatever is written on your card?* Challenge learners to point the arrows on their cards away from the word SIN and, through prayer, to initiate repentance.

8. Close in prayer. Ask the class to pray silently as you slowly read aloud the "Statements of Genuine Repentance" from the last page of Day 5. Pray that God will help learners identify ways they specifically can initiate repentance in their lives.

Requesting Forgiveness

day One

Why Seek Forgiveness?

Angie and Martin had been married nine years when she discovered that he was having an affair with a woman at the office. She gave Martin a choice: "You can't have both of us. The choice is yours." Martin left, but within a week he had come back to say that he wanted to work on the marriage and that he was willing to break off his relationship with Brenda.

A few weeks into the counseling process, Angie was saying, "The thing that bothers me is that Martin is not willing to ask me to forgive him. He said that he is sorry, and I really believe that he has broken off the affair with Brenda."

"It's like you are trying to make me say those words," replied Martin. "I said it was wrong."

"Then why won't you ask me to forgive you?" she pleaded. "I'm willing to forgive you; I want to forgive you. But how can I forgive you when you don't want to be forgiven? It's as though you don't think you need forgiveness because you haven't done anything wrong. I don't understand that."

"I know I did wrong," said Martin. "It's just that asking you to forgive me is so hard." He shook his head. Tears came to his eyes and he said, "I don't know why it's so hard!"

We discovered that there are lots of Angies in the world. When asked, "What do you expect in an apology?" one of every five (21 percent) answered, "I expect him/her to ask for my forgiveness." For them, these were the magic words that indicated sincerity. Their language of apology is *requesting forgiveness*.

Why would requesting forgiveness be so important? Here are the answers we discovered.

Requesting Forgiveness

"Will you please forgive me?"

155

First, requesting forgiveness indicates to some that you want to see the relationship fully restored. When an offense occurs, immediately it creates an emotional barrier between two people. Until that barrier is removed, the relationship cannot go forward. An apology is an attempt to remove the barrier. If you discover that the person's primary apology language is requesting forgiveness, then this is the surest way of removing the barrier. To that person, this is what indicates that you genuinely want to see the relationship restored.

A *second* reason that requesting forgiveness is important is that it shows that you realize you have done something wrong—that you have offended the other person, intentionally or unintentionally. What you said or did may not have been morally wrong. You may even have done or said it in jest. But it offended the other person. He or she now holds it against you. It is an offense that has created a rift between the two of you. In that sense it is wrong, and requesting forgiveness is in order, especially if this is the person's primary apology language.

I met Alma in Tucson. "How do you know that Bob is sincere when he makes an apology?" I asked. "When he says, 'Will you please forgive me?'" responded Alma. She continued, "Saying 'I'm sorry' does not admit guilt in my eyes. My two-year-old says 'I'm sorry' all the time, but when I ask him to say 'Please forgive me,' his eyes get big and he gulps. Asking for forgiveness admits guilt. Even a two-year-old knows this."

Third, requesting forgiveness shows that you are willing to put the future of the relationship in the hands of the offended person. You have admitted your wrong; you have expressed regret; you may have offered to make amends. But now you are saying "Will you forgive me?" You know that you cannot answer that question for that person. It is a choice that he or she must make—to forgive or not to forgive. And the future of the relationship rests on that decision. This takes the control out of your hands, and for some people, this is extremely difficult.

Read Luke 15:11-32. How does the younger son model the importance of "requesting forgiveness" as Dr. Chapman discusses? Record your thoughts in the margin next to the three points above.

How is the response of the elder son similar to the way we sometimes handle the issue of whether or not

to forgive? _____

_____

More often than not, who do you identify with—the younger or elder son? Why?

_____

_____

day Two

Fears and Forgiveness

We were not surprised in our apology research to discover scores of individuals who said, "My spouse almost never apologizes." One husband said, "She's too stubborn to apologize. We've been married ten years, and I've never received an apology from her." A wife said, "I don't know if it's male pride, but he just can't bring himself to apologize unless I give him the silent treatment for a couple of days. He would prefer that both of us be miserable than to admit he is wrong."

So why is requesting forgiveness so important to some people and such a difficult language for others to speak?

WHAT ARE WE AFRAID OF?

Requesting forgiveness is especially difficult for those individuals who have strong controlling personalities. Remember how Martin had so much difficulty in saying the words "Will you please forgive me" to Angie? To ask Angie to forgive him was to relinquish control and put the future of the relationship in her hands. Subconsciously, he found this very difficult.

The fear of rejection is common to humans. None of us like to be rejected. For some people, rejection is almost unbearable. For such individuals, requesting forgiveness is extremely difficult because they know that the forgiveness lies in the hand of the other person, and one of the two choices is not to forgive them, which would be rejection.

Fears and Forgiveness

1. Fear of losing control
2. Fear of rejection
3. Fear of failure

Another fear that sometimes keeps people from requesting forgiveness is the fear of failure. These people typically have a strong moral compass. For them, "doing right" is equated with being good or being successful. Throughout life they have tried to do the right thing. And when they do, they feel successful. To them, admitting wrong is equivalent to admitting, "I am a failure." To admit in human relationships that they have done wrong seems to be admitting failure. Therefore, they find it difficult to admit they are wrong. Typically they will argue vehemently with the other person that what they did was not wrong. They say, "It may have hurt you," or "It may have offended you." "You took it in the wrong way; I didn't mean it that way."

Read again Luke 15:17-21. What did the younger son fear when it came to asking for forgiveness?

_____

_____

OVERCOMING THE FEAR

At a marriage enrichment class, we gave an opportunity for people to ask questions and respond. Lana raised her hand immediately. "As you began to talk about different apology languages, in my mind I said, 'That's us.' My husband will often say 'I'm sorry' and think he is apologizing. But I will say to him, 'You're not apologizing. You're not saying that you're wrong.'

"As you were talking, I realized we've been speaking different languages. He is saying that he's sorry, and to me that's like it's no big deal. I need for him to ask 'Will you forgive me?' because then it feels like he is admitting his wrong and he is asking me to forgive him. It makes it easier for me to forgive and let the thing go. Before tonight it's like we never had closure whenever one of us hurt the other. We talked about it, and we tried to apologize, but it never seemed to be resolved. Later he would say, 'Well, I said I was sorry. Why are you holding on to this? Why can't you get over it?' I didn't know why I couldn't get over it. It's just that it didn't seem right. Now I get it! I'm so glad we came to this class tonight."

Mature people recognize their fears but refuse to be held captive by them. When they value a relationship, they are willing to go against their fears and take the steps necessary to bring healing to the relationship.

The answer lies in acknowledging your fears. You might say something like: "This is one of my fears. This is why I find it difficult to apologize. But I know that no one is perfect, including me. Sometimes I do and say things that offend my spouse or my friend, and it causes a detrimental effect on our relationship. The only way to amend relationships is by apologizing, so I must learn to apologize in spite of my fear. To admit that what I did was wrong doesn't make me a failure. I will admit that I am wrong and I will ask forgiveness."

> "Mature people recognize their fears but refuse to be held captive by them."
> —Gary Chapman

Read I John 4:18. What are the implications of this Scripture as related to the level of "fear" we experience within our relationships?

_____

_____

Generally speaking, how fearful are you when it comes to asking for forgiveness?

Extremely fearful   **Never afraid**

Why do you feel this way?

_____

_____

_____

Request—Don't Demand!

As difficult as it may be for the offender to ask forgiveness, sometimes it's equally difficult for the offender to realize that the offended may not quickly grant it.

There's a vast difference between requesting forgiveness and demanding forgiveness. In our research, we continually encountered individuals who expected, yes, even demanded that the offended party forget the offense and move on. One wife said, "I can hear it now in my head. I've heard it hundreds of times through our twenty-five years of marriage. He insists, 'I said "I'm sorry." What more do you want?' I just wish that one time he would look me in the eyes and say, 'Will you please forgive me?' He demands my forgiveness, but he never apologizes, and he never changes anything."

Don't demand forgiveness. You cannot expect it. When we demand forgiveness, we fail to understand the nature of forgiveness. Forgiveness is essentially a choice to lift the penalty and to let the person back into our lives. It is to pardon the offense so that we might redevelop trust. Forgiveness says, "I care about our relationship. Therefore, I choose to accept your apology and no longer demand justice." It is essentially a gift. A gift that is demanded is no longer a gift.

Read again Luke 15:21-32. How does the parable of the lost son reveal the "gift" nature of forgiveness? Record your thoughts in the margin.

NOT A SMALL THING

Please understand that when you request to be forgiven, you are making a huge request. It will be costly to the persons you have offended. When they forgive you, they must give up their desire for justice. They must relinquish their hurt and anger, their feeling of embarrassment or humiliation.

They must give up their feelings of rejection and betrayal. Sometimes, they must live with the consequences of your wrong behavior.

Because of the costliness of forgiveness, don't expect the offended person to forgive you immediately. If the offense is minor and if you apologize in the primary apology language of the offended person, then perhaps his or her forgiveness may be extended rather quickly. But if the offense is major and often repeated, it will take time for the offended party to process your apology, especially if that person's apology language is the language of restitution or repentance. It takes time to see if you will follow through on making restitution or genuinely repenting and changing destructive behaviors. The person must be convinced of your sincerity, and that may well take time.

Review the statements found in the margin. These statements may help you learn to speak the apology language of requesting forgiveness. Check samples that resonate what you need to say to someone you love. Pray for God's strength to help you initiate the request to be forgiven.

day *Four*

Discovering Apology Languages

We have introduced you to the five languages of an apology—five ways to express your apology. One of these five languages speaks more deeply to us of sincerity than the other four. You may appreciate hearing all five languages, but if you don't hear your primary apology language, you will question the sincerity of the apologizer. On the other hand, if the apology is expressed in your primary language, then you will find it much easier to forgive the offender.

Therefore, it is extremely important to discover your primary apology language and the primary language of the significant people in your life. This will enhance your ability to both give and receive effective apologies.

STATEMENTS REQUESTING FORGIVENESS

❑ I'm sorry for the way I spoke to you. I know it was loud and harsh. You didn't deserve that. It was very wrong of me, and I want to ask you to forgive me.

❑ I know that what I did hurt you very deeply. You have every right never to speak to me again, but I am truly sorry for what I did. And I hope that you can find it in your heart to forgive me.

❑ I didn't intend to hurt you but obviously I have. I realize that now, and I see that my actions were wrong even though I was just trying to have fun. It's never right to have fun if someone gets hurt. I promise you I will try never to do that again. And I want to ask you if you will please forgive me.

QUESTIONS FOR IDENTIFYING YOUR OWN LANGUAGE OF APOLOGY

First, we want to help you discover your own apology language—the one you would most like to hear when you are offended. Some individuals will know immediately their own primary language of apology. For others, it will not be that easy. Ask yourself the following questions:

Expressing Regret
"I am sorry."

Accepting Responsibility
"I was wrong."

Making Restitution
"What can I do to make it right?"

Requesting Forgiveness
"Will you please forgive me?"

Genuinely Repenting
"I'll try not to do that again."

Question 1: What do I expect the person to say or do that would make it possible for me to genuinely forgive him or her? You may find that your answer will involve several apology languages.

Question 2: What hurts most deeply about this situation? This question is especially helpful if the offender has not yet apologized at all or has not apologized to your satisfaction.

Question 3: When I apologize to others, which of the five languages do I think is most important? This question is based on the assumption that the apology language you speak to others is probably the language you would most wish to receive.

ARE YOU BILINGUAL?

Answering the previous three questions will probably enable you to determine your primary apology language. Actually, it is quite common that two or three of the apology languages will be rather important to you. But typically one stands out above the others. However, when you ask yourself which is more important, and you hear yourself say, *Well, really they are all important,* then perhaps you are bilingual.

Suggestion:

If you and your spouse are completing this study together, set aside time to discuss each other's apology language. Talk about the words you need to say to effectively apologize in the other person's apology language.

Take time to think about the three questions above. Identify your apology language. Describe any "bilingual" tendencies in yourself.

_____

_____

_____

SPEAKING A DIFFERENT LANGUAGE

As we looked at our apology survey data from couples, we reviewed the extent that a husband and wife matched in their primary apology languages. We found that a full 75 percent of the couples differed in their most preferred apology language. If you apologize to your spouse in the way that you most want to be apologized to, our data suggest that, on average, you wouldn't stumble upon his or her favorite apology language until your third attempt! Assuming the survey is accurate, that means three of every four couples must learn to speak an apology language different from the one they most want to hear!

How then do you discover the primary apology language of other people with whom you have a relationship? If they are willing to discuss this study, introduce them to the three previous questions. If they are not willing to do this study themselves, it might take some detective work. Use the three questions (plus a bonus question) found in the margin. The answers people give to these questions, reframed for conversation, will most likely reveal their primary apology language.

SPEAKING ALL FIVE LANGUAGES

Please don't hear us saying that you should speak only the primary apology language of the other person. What we are saying is that you want to be certain that you speak the other person's primary apology language. Then you can sprinkle in the other four languages and get additional emotional credit. But without the primary language, the other languages may not communicate your sincerity. In fact, when you don't know someone's apology language, then you should seek to cover all of your bases. If you genuinely speak each of the five apology languages, you are bound to hit upon something that will be music to the offended person's ears, who will then sense that your apology is sincere.

Practice expressing an apology in an apology language other than your primary one.

_____

_____

Three questions to help discover another person's Apology Language

1. Ask: *Describe an apology that someone once gave you that you considered insufficient. What was lacking?*

2. When you realize you have offended someone, ask: *It hurts me that I have hurt you. Why don't you tell me what hurts you most about what I said or did?*

3. Ask: *When you express an apology to someone for something you have done that hurt him or her, what do you think is the most important part of an apology?*

Bonus question: If you are not yet sure, add this question, with its built-in compliment: *I value our relationship. What do I need to do or say in order for you to consider forgiving me?*

163

day *Five*

Apologizing to Yourself

Jordan was in my office crying—sobbing would be a better word. I have known him for all of his eighteen years, but I had never seen him this emotionally disturbed. In short, he was the all-American model teenager. "I've really blown it," he said. "I've messed up my whole life. I really wish I could die." With those three statements, I knew he was in serious trouble.

Jordan had become involved with a young woman who became pregnant. The week before she had undergone an abortion. His whole body was shaking. Tears were falling on his jeans like rain. He said, "I let my parents down. I let God down. I let myself down. I let her down. I just wish I could die."

Jordan was young, but he was wise enough to know that he needed help. For the next twelve months I saw him regularly. I watched him step up to the plate and apologize to his parents, to the young woman, and to her mother. I saw him weep as he acknowledged to God that he had sinned and asked for His forgiveness. Near the end of our year of counseling (he was now a freshman in college), Jordan said to me, "I think there is one more apology I need to make."

"What's that?" I asked.

"I think I need to apologize to myself."

"That's interesting. Why would you say that?"

"I keep beating myself up," he said. "I keep remembering what I did and feeling bad about it. I don't think I have ever forgiven myself. Everybody else seems to have forgiven me—but I haven't forgiven me. Maybe if I could apologize to myself, I could forgive myself."

WHO WE ARE—WHO WE WANT TO BE

Why would you apologize to yourself? In a general sense, you apologize to yourself for the same reason you apologize to someone else: You want to restore the relationship. When you apologize to yourself, you are seeking to remove the emotional disequilibrium between the person you want to be (the ideal self) and the person you are (the real self).

Read 2 Corinthians 5:17-21. How does this Scripture relate to our tendency to "beat ourselves up" over mistakes? What hope does this Scripture offer?

_____

_____

HOW DO I APOLOGIZE TO MYSELF?

When it comes to apologizing to yourself, we like to encourage audible self-talk. If you are aware of your own primary apology language, then focus on speaking that language, but include the other four languages for additional emotional credit.

We suggest that you write out your self-apology before you speak it to yourself. Below is a summary of the apology that Jordan made to himself. We have removed his name and left the blanks so you can include your name. You may change the order of his statements, and you may change the wording. We offer it simply to help you get started in forming your self-apology. We believe that apologizing to yourself is an important step in the process of restoring "peace with yourself."

Write your self-apology statement. After you have written it, stand in front of the mirror, look yourself in the eyes, and audibly give your apology to yourself.

"_____, I want to tell you that I did wrong; I mean really wrong, grossly wrong. _____, I want to tell you how bad I feel about it and how much I regret what I did. I want to tell you that I have learned my lesson. _____, I want to give myself the freedom to be happy again. And, _____, I want to ask you to forgive me and to help me make the most of my life in the future. _____, because I believe your apology is sincere, I choose to forgive you."

WHAT IF WE ALL LEARNED TO APOLOGIZE EFFECTIVELY?

The art of apologizing is not easy, but it can be learned, and it is worth the effort. Apologizing opens up a whole new world of emotional and spiritual health.

"The righteous cry out, and the LORD hears, and delivers them from all their troubles. The LORD is near the brokenhearted; He saves those crushed in spirit" (Ps. 34:17-18, HCSB).

Read Psalm 34:17-18, printed in the margin. Underline the blessings you can receive when you humble yourself in apology.

Having apologized, we are able to look ourselves in the mirror, look people in the eyes, and worship God "in spirit and in truth."

If apologizing were a way of life, no walls would be built. Relationships would be authentic. Certainly people would fail, but the failures would be dealt with in an open and honest manner. Regret would be expressed; responsibility would be accepted. Restitution would be made. Genuine repentance would be our intention, and we would stand humbly and say, "I need somebody to forgive me." We believe in most cases if we learned to apologize effectively, we would be genuinely forgiven.

As a concluding exercise, consider the people involved in the different areas of your life whom you have probably hurt. How can you apply the languages of apology to all aspects of your life? Below, write out your thoughts. After reflecting, commit yourself to God through prayer. Ask Him to empower you as the one to make the first effort in apologizing and restoring relationships in your life.

_____

_____

_____

_____

Before the Session

Bring both a spray bottle of glass cleaning solution and paper towels.

During the Session

1. As you begin the class, clean a surface in your room. Call attention to the fifth apology language [requesting forgiveness, p. 155]. Ask: *How is forgiveness like cleaning a dirty surface? How is it different?* Explain that asking for forgiveness is a deeply spiritual exercise. It reaches into the depth of our hearts as we seek to be forgiven for what we have admittedly done wrong. Ask: *Why is it difficult to say, "Will you please forgive me?" What does our request for forgiveness insinuate about ourselves?*

2. Read Luke 15:11-32. Discuss: *The younger son found himself desperate and broken. Do you think the younger son was fully open to being forgiven?* Emphasize that the younger son didn't really expect to be fully restored. He was nervous. Ask: *How does the younger son's anxiety parallel anxiety we feel when we approach someone with a request to be forgiven?*

3. Explain that Dr. Chapman discusses three reasons why forgiveness is important. Ask: *What three reasons were listed? Can you think of any other reasons forgiveness is important?* Discuss the activities on pages 156 and 157.

4. Ask: *What are some reasons we typically fear asking for forgiveness? Why do we have these fears?* Review the list of fears listed in the margin of Day 2 (p. 158). Refer learners back to Luke 15:17-21. Call for responses to the activity on page 158. Invite someone to read aloud 1 John 4:18. Ask: *How does this passage speak to our level of fear within relationships?* Ask learners to share their responses from the last activity on Day 2 about their level of fear when asking forgiveness.

5. Emphasize that forgiveness is like a gift. When someone pardons you, it is a big deal! Ask learners to give their responses to the first activity on Day 3. Explain that requesting forgiveness has everything to do with humbling oneself. You have to admit you did something wrong and make yourself vulnerable to the person you hurt. Review the "Statements for Requesting Forgiveness" as a class. Ask learners to share how they responded to the last activity on Day 3.

6. Explain that it is important to discover your primary apology language and to recognize the apology languages that are vital to the person to whom you need to apologize. Ask learners if they were able to determine their apology languages using the three questions in Day 4. For further discussion, encourage learners to share their experiences of identifying the apology languages of significant others in their lives using the reframed questions found in the margin of page 163. Clarify any doubts that learners have about all of these questions.

7. Emphasize that we often have a combination of apology languages. This was described in Day 4 as being "bilingual." Ask: *Did you discover in yourself or your loved one any bilingual tendencies?* Ask: *Why do you suppose utilizing all five languages of apology is a good idea?* Finally, ask learners to share how they responded to the final activity on Day 4.

8. Ask: *Why do you suppose an apology to yourself is a good idea? Typically, is this easy or hard for you to do? Why?* Read aloud 1 Corinthians 5:17. Admitting our mistakes can get us down and affect our self-esteem if we don't remember that dealing with sin and apologizing are ways that God continues to work out His creative transformation within us. Refer to the bottle of cleaning solution you used earlier. Explain that we must remember that God is spiritually cleaning up our lives, washing the sin-stain out of our lives. Apologizing to ourselves is healthy, because we are acknowledging that we deserve better—we deserve God's creative work in our lives! Challenge learners to fill out the "self-apology statement" on page 165. Emphasize that no matter your apology language, this step can complete the apology process.

9. Conclude the study by asking learners to review their reactions to the last activity on Day 5. Ask someone to read aloud Psalm 34:17-18. Emphasize that the Lord draws near to those who humble themselves. Challenge learners to find strength in the Lord as they seek to exercise the five languages of apology in their relationships. Allow a few moments so that learners may prayer silently. Close in a prayer for each learner. Encourage members to pray for each other in the coming weeks.

10. Announce the new *MasterWork* study based on Ephesians 4 by Chip Ingram titled *The Miracle of Life Change* that begins next week. Remind learners to be prepared for the group session by reading the lesson and filling in the interactive exercises.